# INTO INDIA

# INTO INDIA

*John Keay*

Charles Scribner's Sons

NEW YORK

1 3 5 7 9 11 13 15 17 19 I/C 20 18 16 14 12 10 8 6 4 2

Printed in Great Britain
Library of Congress Catalog Card Number 74-29554
ISBN 0-684-14237-6

# FOR JULIA

# CONTENTS

vii

# ILLUSTRATIONS

# ACKNOWLEDGEMENTS

It would be a hopeless task to acknowledge all those who have contributed information used in this book. From a succession of faces and half-forgotten names I remember with pleasure Dr. A. P. Singh, Hoshang and Almitra Patel, Mr. and Mrs. Y. N. Krishnamurthy, Ammu and Abu Abraham, Dilip Mukherji, Ghulam Mohammed Major, Mr. M. Peter, Doctors Peter Snell, Donald Duck and Marie Mitchell, Mr. Peter Rogerson, Fr. Cronin S.J., Ma Talyarkhan, Ruth Prawer Jhabvala, Raj Krishna and James Nicholson.

Particular mention should be made of those friends who, besides sharing their knowledge of India, were prepared to accommodate two often bedraggled travellers, namely Girish Karnad and family, Vasant and Sunanda Karnad, Timothy and Tricia Lankester, Kranti Singh and Christina Noble. To Christina and my sister Pat I owe my love of India and the chance to indulge it so often over the last seven years.

Simon Ricketts, Anthony Hacking, John R. Murray and, once again, Christina Noble have made helpful and, more important, encouraging comments on the text.

To the books I have consulted only a long bibliography could do justice; India has fascinated not a few writers. Some of those I have found most useful are mentioned in the text and footnotes, whilst a select bibliography for those interested in further reading is given at the end.

Finally, or almost, a word of thanks to the Indian people. They are their own worst critics and nothing sells there like another attack on India. Unsympathetic works call forth an official rejection and then become best-sellers. This little book is not unsympathetic and scarcely deserves such notoriety or success. But there are, I am sure, errors and criticisms for both of which I accept full responsibility. The Indian public have never resented my curiosity in the way that I so often have theirs. I thank them in advance for showing the same traditional forbearance wherever the text is unfair to them.

To my wife this work is dedicated. She has both followed me and accompanied me to India. Together we have travelled tens of thousands of miles there. In the course of them she married me. She has helped with every page of this book and has then typed it. My little dedication is as nothing compared to hers.

# GLOSSARY

| | |
|---|---|
| *adivasi* | aboriginal or tribal. |
| *ahimsa* | non-violence, a Jain concept reinterpreted as a political doctrine by Mahatma Gandhi. |
| *ashram* | a monastery catering for lay visitors or pilgrims. |
| *babu* | someone who works behind a desk or aspires to some authority. |
| *bourka* | the voluminous outer layer of black silk fitted with eye-slits worn by orthodox Muslim ladies observing *purdah*. |
| *chaukidar* | a caretaker or night watchman. |
| *darshan* | the meretricious encountering of a saint or celebrity. |
| *dhobi* | a laundryman. |
| *dhoti* | a length of white cloth ingeniously tied and worn as the traditional Indian equivalent of trousers. |
| *ghats* | steps up from a river or any steep embankment. Hence mountains like the Western Ghats. |
| *ghi* | clarified butter, most prized of the cow's five products and the essential cooking agent in Indian *haute cuisine*. |
| *gopuram* | the massive and intricately sculptured gateway of a South Indian temple. |
| *guru* | a religious leader in the case of the Sikhs. More generally any religious mentor or confessor. |
| *harijan* | Mahatma Gandhi's euphemism for an Untouchable. |
| *jati* | the word for caste in contemporary India, particularly the sub-caste. |
| *jauhar* | the Rajput ritual of defeat when the men march forth to certain death whilst their women throw themselves on a funeral pyre. |
| *khaddi* | homespun cloth or cotton usually of a natural colour. |
| *kurta* | long tunic shirt, often white, worn throughout India. |
| *lungi* | like a *dhoti* only more simply tied, usually coloured, and worn particularly in the south. |
| *mandapam* | central shrine of a Jain or Hindu temple. |
| *mullah* | Muslim religious and social leader. |
| *muni* | a monk, usually Jain. |

# Glossary

*puja*     any Hindu act of worship or prayer.

*purdah*     literally a curtain but commonly the seclusion in which a good Muslim keeps his womenfolk.

*saddhu*     a wandering mendicant supposedly devoted to religious self-discipline but often rather disreputable.

*sati*     the ritual burning of a widow on the death of her husband. It has been banned for well over a century.

*sannyasi*     a wandering ascetic who has renounced the cares of this world in preparation for death.

*sikhara*     the short temple spire found mostly in northern India.

*stupa* (or *tope*)     early Buddhist mausoleum

*swami*     Hindu religious or caste leader.

*tilaka* (or *tikka*)     forehead mark of red paste worn by married Hindu ladies.

*varna*     the Vedic word for caste signifying the four traditional castes of Brahmins, Kshatriyas, Vaisyas and Sudras.

# INTRODUCTION

> INDIA, INDIES . . . Some have imagined that the
> name of the land of *Nod* ('wandering'), to which
> Cain is said to have migrated and which has the same
> consonants,* is but a form of this; which is worth
> noting, as this idea may have had to do with the
> curious statement in some medieval writers that
> certain Eastern races were the descendants of Cain.
>
> *Hobson-Jobson, A glossary of colloquial*
> *Anglo-Indian words and phrases.*

I can add no more to the derivation of Nod but if Cain was really
the first visitor to India he deserves to be commemorated here.
This book is written for people who have visited, will visit or
would like to visit India. In a land where the unfamiliar is often
shocking, the confusion baffling and the grotesque nauseating, an
introduction, even if it serves only to alert the unsuspecting, is
essential.

In the last six years I have spent many months travelling in India
but have never lived there. I have seen India and come to love it
but always as an outsider. Obviously there is a disadvantage here.
I can lay no claim to the profound insight which comes of direct
involvement. My generation of Englishmen has no particular axe
to grind where India is concerned. But this makes it possible to
see the country from the outside, to interpret it from the dispassionate, objective viewpoint which is typically that of the
tourist and traveller.

In these months of travelling I have been lucky enough to see
almost the whole of India. A country so vast and varied gets a
grip on you, drawing you away from the few cities to the small
towns, the villages and the open countryside. Dust and distance

---

* i.e. 'n' and 'd' as in Indus, India, Sind and Hindu.

I

become constant companions. In the Land of Nod wandering is still an obsession. Holy men and hippies, saints and salesmen, musicians and politicians—a whole army of itinerants spend their days wandering round India. Mahatma Gandhi owed his understanding and love of the Indian masses to a willingness to embrace the life of the road, or at least the railways. Anyone prepared to undergo a similar baptism of dust may expect to acquire something of this understanding and affection: and in the process will no doubt cease to distinguish between them. For it is a fact about India that however dispassionate one's approach, it never for long remains so.

Elsewhere in the entry quoted above Hobson-Jobson declares that no Englishman who has had to do with India ever speaks of a man of that country as 'an Indian'. The same could be said of most Indians. A man is a Bengali or a Tamil, a Sikh or a Parsi, a Brahmin or an Untouchable before he is an Indian. The point was well illustrated by a 'Ugandan Asian' I met while writing this book. He was a Patel of Bania caste from Kaira in Gujerat. As one would expect of a Bania he had been in business, wholesale, and was, an educated, responsible and until a few days before, prosperous member of Ugandan society. I asked him whether most of the Ugandan Asians were Gujeratis. Far from it, there were Punjabi Sikhs, Goanese Christians, Malayali teachers, Khoja Muslims and so on. All of them were as much strangers to him as the Ugandan Africans. Being lumped together either as Indians or Ugandan Asians was not helping anyone to understand their particular problems, to make them feel welcome and understood or to accommodate their particular aptitudes.

For one country, one nation, India has more races, more languages, more religions and more social groups (tribes and castes) than any comparable corner of the globe. This incredible diversity of peoples is one of the country's great fascinations. To understand not just its society but its history, architecture, institutions and politics it is essential to resolve some of this confusion. The gruesome Towers of Silence in Bombay or the delicate marble temples of Mount Abu are meaningless without some knowledge of the Parsis and Jains, of their significance to India's history and their role in modern society. Equally meaningless are the Indian press and the political scene without some idea of the connexion between the Untouchables and the Republican Party of India or the Maharajas and the Swatantra Party.

Unlike the prophets of doom (with whom India has long acquaintance) it is not intended by this emphasis on the diversity of the country to suggest that there is an imminent danger of its disintegration or that there is no such thing as an Indian. The Indian characteristics of India are in many ways less tangible. There is, of course, the constitution and the nationhood it embodies, both the products of a long and largely united struggle for independence. But more important there is an Indian way of life, Indian attitudes and Indian obsessions. Regardless of their community Indians are recognisable as a gentle, excitable and slightly potty people. The land of Nod is characterised by a certain passivity interpreted, according to one's point of view, as lethargic resignation or tolerant stoicism. There are pan-Indian institutions like the railways, the rest houses, democracy and the monsoon. And most important of all there is the national obsession with religion. For most people this means Hinduism, a peculiarly Indian phenomenon tantamount to the Indian way of life. The mass of non-Hindu communities owe to it a good deal more than they care to admit.

Two features of Indian society, to many the most distinctive, I have not dealt with in great detail. I am thinking of, on the one hand, poverty and, on the other, the progress being made in the battle against it. 'We are a poor country' declares a character in R. K. Narayan's *The English Teacher*. These words one hears over and over again in India. Asked if I like the country I say yes. 'But how can you be liking this place.We are such a poor country.' The poverty is obvious and if for one minute one should question it there is a mass of statistics to prove it. Twenty-eight million unemployed, an average weekly wage of fifty pence, sixty million living at below subsistence level and so on. Even to question the figures is to lay oneself open to accusations of callousness.

But take any street scene in Calcutta. There is a man selling combs, matches or shoelaces and beside him there is a beggar with nothing but his deformity. Each clears about one rupee a day. To the statistician the salesman is employed, the beggar unemployed. There is no school-leaving age, no unemployment benefit and no old age pension so how can one assess unemployment? What are the criteria and can one make any valid comparison with figures for a country in the West? What too of the fifty pence weekly wage? In a good hotel it might cover breakfast for one. In the bazaar it might buy ten substantial meals and in the hands of a shrewd mother it can be made to feed a family of three for a week. If, as is usual, she as well as her husband and maybe even an older child are also earning they might even run to two substantial meals a day. But probably they won't because a simple diet is more to their taste and the few extra rupees are, in their book, better spent on a new set of bangles for mother and the girls.

Real poverty is seldom quite as obvious as it seems. Outside the big cities most Indian men wear loose white clothes. By European standards they look shapeless and tattered. In fact they are extremely practical and no indication at all of what the wearer is worth. The tragedies are there all right, hardship, squalor, degradation, but much of what first strikes the visitor as appalling is only so by Western standards; by Indian standards it may be quite acceptable. To understand India it is important to appreciate the Indian point of view. If the theme of India's poverty is not present on every page of this book it is because by most its existence is taken for granted. Even this is not callousness; only after coming to terms with the tragic is the experience of India possible and enjoyable.

By way of balancing the record I have largely ignored the progressive side of contemporary India. The country is, of course, in the throes of an unprecedented economic and educational revolution. India could well be the miracle of the century, the Japan of the 'eighties. Urbanisation and education, even just literacy, may well dismantle the caste system, destroy Hinduism and usher in a true welfare state. The country I know may well be unrecognisable in another twenty years. There is a certain fascination in tracing the cracks as they begin to appear in the traditional fabric of Indian society. Watch them closely and they become alive and enthralling. But stand back and they become insignificant, almost invisible, against the massive bulk of tradition. In India things happen slowly. Untouchability has been abolished for twenty-five years. Instead of fifty million Untouchables there are now seventy-five million ex-Untouchables of whom nine-tenths are no better off than before. Neither disintegration nor revolution nor the great leap forward come as quickly as the pundits predict. Books about India as it is, tend to be up to date for longer than those which try to anticipate what it may become.

India has a curious way of changing people. The authoritarian becomes a bully and the earnest student an emaciated ascetic. No one comes away indifferent. You feel either rejected or converted and the most balanced subsequent analysis soon plunges into bitter recriminations or soars with extravagant praise. India is never just a country or a holiday; it is a whole experience. It asks much of visitors and by their response to it they judge it. India is what it makes of you. For this bit of self-discovery as well as for the country's more obvious surprises it is as well to be prepared.

# I. FIRST IMPRESSIONS

## *Delhi and the Punjab*

Long before sighting Bombay the P. & O. passengers used dutifully to record in their journals the first gentle hint of India, a balmy waft of sweet spicy air haunting the foredeck. In Delhi clambering on swollen feet from jet to tarmac there is no such gentle acclimatisation. One of the richest, strangest and most exciting smells imaginable shoots up the nostrils like a whiff of brandy. Urine and jasmine, cow dung smoke and frangipani, low octane exhaust and the acrid bidi cigarette combine with the baffling aromas of Indian cuisine to make the air almost tangible. In the quiet, cool expectancy of the post monsoon dawn this smell can be either wildly upsetting or immensely reassuring; it all depends on whether India is a new or a familiar experience. More picquant for an added whiff of pine resin or drying fish, the smell is still there on a chilly night in the Himalayas or under the shade of a coconut palm on the Malabar coast. It pervades the whole subcontinent testifying to a way of life and to a tradition peculiarly Indian.

Much the same could be said of the confused little scenes which comprise every visitor's first impressions. A man wrapping a seemingly endless length of cotton round his head, another pulling a spade while his mate pushes it, a child peeing in the gutter, squatting figures in the fields donating their 'night soil' as manure, an unbelievably beautiful girl eating a roast corn cob. The little vignettes pile up on one another as the taxi rattles down the middle of the road into Delhi. It's like a Breughel painting, so many unrelated things going on everywhere. High in an outlandish-looking tree monkeys cascade through the branches, underneath a family are cooking their breakfast. Here comes a

7

cart pulled by two lumbering buffalo; on the cart a mountain of new air-conditioners with the driver wrapped in a blanket and apparently asleep. The shops, if they are shops, look like temporary creations of the fairground, wooden shacks with no plate glass and no door. Such buildings as one sees seem to be only half complete and of a distinctly 'forties style with lots of curly wrought iron and frosted glass. There is a general untidiness about the place, piles of builders' rubble and farmyard refuse both off and on the road.

Unfamiliar as most of it is, a British visitor is nagged by a *déjà vu* feeling. The post boxes are red, the Ambassador taxi is surely related to the old Morris Oxford and everywhere there are advertisements for Wills Gold Flake and Capstan. From the bedside radio in your hotel room comes the unbelievable voice of Melvin de Melho with the eight o'clock news. All India Radio it is, but you will be forgiven if you think it Alvar Liddell and the B.B.C.

Outside life teems everywhere. Not just people but animals, birds, flowers, insects. Crows that caw and stare and caw and stare, little squirrels that infest every tree, big heavy centipedes, ants of every size and description, enormous articulated wasps, phosphorescent house lizards, spiders, frogs, beetles, gigantic moths, winged grasshoppers, brilliant fluttering birds and enormous brown kites which swoop within inches of your *al fresco* breakfast. The exotic and the unspeakable are everywhere cheek by jowl. A hoopoe flashing its golden crown pecks beside a pye dog with sagging tits and fly-blown eyes, an elegant white egret perches on the mud-spattered back of a monstrously ugly buffalo. Even without the six hundred million people and their millions of cows, goats and sheep there would be precious little privacy.

Fortunately privacy is not something which Indians value. No streets in the world are as crowded as those of Calcutta, Bombay and Old Delhi. Not just the pavements but the road itself is alive with people, so many and at first glance so alike in their shapeless white clothes, that one is revolted. To stand at 9.30 a.m. on

London Bridge and watch the well-drilled phalanx of suited city workers thunder over the Thames is an impressive sight. But the crowds in India are different. Their apparent lack of purpose and discipline, their unco-ordinated chaos is as disturbing as the teeming confusion of a flattened ant hill. As with the smells the challenge is one of analysis. Once you can identify the cloying sweetness of jasmine or the not unpleasant smoke of burning cow dung the air becomes friendly and exciting. Once you can distinguish the sweet seller and the fortune teller, the Brahmin and the Untouchable, the Tamil and the Punjabi these very crowds start to dissolve and you glory in the diversity and excitement of the Indian concourse. It makes the uniformed army of London Bridge seem dull beyond reason.

For the unsuspecting visitor there are a number of hurdles to be cleared before he can start to enjoy these sort of scenes. First, he must forget about the invention of the lavatory and the bathroom. Heading for the Himalayas you awake in your first-class sleeper as the train bowls across the Punjab. You throw up the blinds to welcome the sun rising over the lush countryside but the excitement is rudely shattered by a row of bare bottoms lining the track and of crouching figures deep in the cornfields. With the regularity of clockwork the bowels of a nation are on the move. The women were out before dawn; sunrise is the hour for the men. By the time your breakfast has arrived 600 million Indians have made their contribution to the countryside. I have seen a party's entire election manifesto devoted to what the nation should and should not do with its 'night soil'. No doubt the national product could be put to better use but in the countryside at least no one particularly wants to change their habits. If there was a lavatory no one would use it. It is both more pleasant and more correct to squat with your friends as the sun rises and the train rumbles by.

Secondly, the visitor must come to accept the spitting and expectoration, the scratching of any part of the body that irritates or the staring at anything that fascinates. When a man having examined you at length makes a guttural noise like the last of the bath water running away, spits with apparent venom and starts scratching his genitals, try not to flinch; he may still entertain the highest opinion of you.

Hardest of all one must learn to distinguish between what in all this is by Indian standards acceptable and what is true poverty, hardship and squalor. How does one enjoy such a place without becoming totally indifferent to hardship? Everywhere there are beggars, pretty little children who follow you for hours, legless old men on trolleys who scud along the roadside like crabs, hideous old hags or young girls with a baby at the breast. Each has to offer for your curiosity some malformation or tragic appeal. Indulge your curiosity and you will be expected to pay for it—and will probably be pestered until you do. Everything, even a freak show, has a price. By looking at misfortune you humiliate. The least you can do is help alleviate it. But ignore a beggar completely and you will rarely be pestered. Unfortunately it is not just a question of not looking. Beggars are adept at catching one's attention. Little hands tug at your sleeve, arms thin as axe handles bar your path, bent old men call you plaintively. 'Sahib', 'Bara Sahib',★ 'Babuji',† 'Sir', 'Maharaja', even 'Judge'. (That I couldn't resist; worth four annas any day.) Only after repeatedly walking grandly away from porters and taxi-drivers demanding over the odds does one begin to cultivate that look of stern indifference calculated to dishearten even the most persistent mendicant.

On just two occasions have beggars, sound of limb and of working age, stopped me. One was a French student in Goa, the other a 'campus saddhu' in Kashmir. Indians have more dignity. The man with nothing in which to indulge your curiosity is unlikely to be begging. And probably the more deformed the beggar the more successful he is. Total hardship is not so flamboyant or obvious. It is in the failure of a whole village's crops somewhere in north-eastern Uttar Pradesh which never even reaches the papers, in the death of a herdsman's only cow, in the

★ i.e. a big or great Sahib.
† A *babu* is anyone who lives by his wits rather than as a labourer.

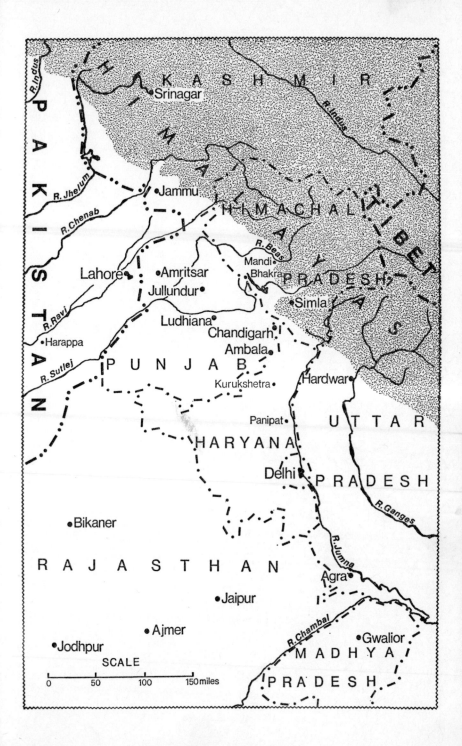

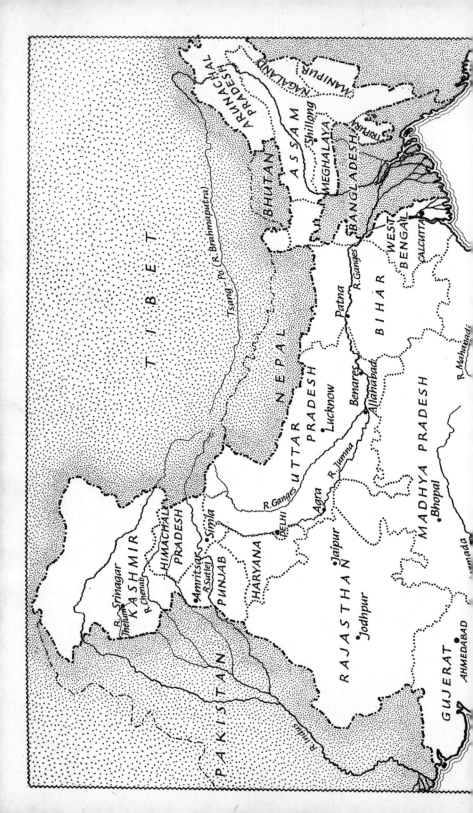

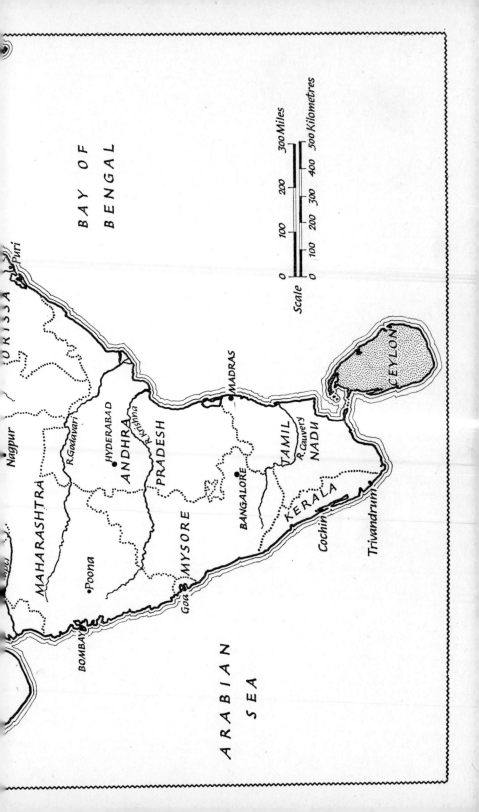

loss of her husband for a girl of twenty with four children and less than the price of a railway ticket to her own village.

There are two concepts, *karma* and *dharma*, which are so basic to every Hindu that he would be pushed to define them. *Karma* is the relationship between one's actions in one incarnation and one's station in the next while *dharma* is the yardstick by which one's actions are judged. Everything has a *dharma*. For the river its *dharma* is to flow, for the seed to grow, for the beggar to beg and for the soldier to fight. A man's performance in this life is judged by how closely he follows the dictates and traditions of his particular *dharma*. By the law of *karma* this will determine his station in his next reincarnation. In other words quite apart from the economic catastrophe of a cowman losing his cow or a wife her husband they face the much worse danger of forsaking their *dharma*. For the cowman there is no question of his taking up roadwork. Far better he sells all and borrows the rest at a ruinous interest rate to get another cow. For the rest of this life he and his family will struggle at subsistence level but at least he will stand a better chance in the next.

Perhaps this accounts for the apparent cheerfulness or at least the lack of depression amongst Indians. For all the poverty and hardship Indians are a jollier bunch than their counterparts in the West. Neuroses are as rare amongst businessmen as bitterness is amongst beggars. Suicide is exceptional and the *angst* of our Western world unknown. A long face reserved for the plight of India is best forgotten if one is to cope with the more typically Indian characteristic of boundless optimism.

\*     \*     \*

Amidst the milling crowds anywhere in Delhi one figure soon begins to stand out. He wears a neatly tied turban with no loose ends, he has a beard often rolled round a piece of what looks like elastic, a fine moustache and, on his wrist, a steel bracelet. The first time you see him he is probably driving a taxi. His name, or one of them anyway, is Singh. He comes from the Punjab and he is a Sikh. That much is certain for virtually all Sikhs and only Sikhs wear such a turban, all Sikhs are called Singh (though not all Singhs are Sikhs), all Sikhs come from the Punjab and all Delhi taxi-drivers are Sikhs. There is no community in India so easily distinguished. Even Sikh women usually stick to the traditional Punjabi dress which, unlike the one-piece sari worn by most other Indian women, consists of two closely fitting garments, a long narrow tunic and trousers as calf hugging as ballet tights.

The Sikhs, pronounced 'seeks' or more correctly 'sicks' though referred to familiarly as 'Sardarjis', are not a race or caste but a religious order. By Indian standards they are of comparatively recent origin. They revere a succession of *Gurus*, religious leaders, starting with Nanak (d. 1538) and ending with Govind Singh (d. 1708) and a holy book, the Granth, in which their teachings are enshrined. The sixteenth and seventeenth centuries in India saw Mohammedanism at its peak. Though influenced by its teachings, Sikhism was a reformed Hinduism, shorn of caste and inspired by the need to resist Muslim persecution. In 1675 Govind Singh's father was executed by the Muslims. The gauntlet was down and Sikh resistance quickly took on a more militant character. The last Guru initiated his followers, the *Khalsa* (Pure), into what was more an army than a religion. Their uniform, worn to this day by all good Sikhs, consisted of the five *kakkars**—the steel bracelet, a wooden comb, short underpants, a small knife and a vow never to cut their hair. Underneath the tightly wrapped turban every good Sardarji should have a pile of long black hair which has never known the scissors.

The turban was adopted simply for convenience but in a country where every fold of the sari has some social significance it seems strange that the colour of the Sikh turban, maroon, green, black or red, is simply a question of personal taste. Yet I have never heard any other explanation. The only exceptions seem to be the white ones worn by the Namdari sect and the

---

* The Punjabi words for the comb, the bracelet and so on all begin with the letter 'k', that is *kakkar*. Each kakkar has its particular connotation. The uncut hair is for holiness, the iron comb for poverty, the bangle for eternity, the knife for militancy and the short pants for modesty.

powder blue shade which is worn only by Akalis. As a highly militant brotherhood, the Sikhs *raison d'être* was the overthrowing of Islam and in this the cream of their forces, equivalents of the crusading knights, were the Akalis. In Amritsar, the Rome of the Sikhs with its St. Peter's, the Golden Temple, the blue turbans are still common, though it would be surprising, even alarming, to find one of these warriors behind the wheel of a taxi.

Although the Sikhs along with the British and the Mahrattas played their part in precipitating the collapse of Muslim empire in India their hour of glory came not in the eighteenth but the nineteenth century. In 1797 a remarkable little man, blind in one eye, passionately devoted to horses and obsessed with the idea of uniting the Sikh clans became Governor of Lahore. He was Ranjit Singh, Sher e Punjab (the Lion of the Punjab). In forty years he created an empire reaching from Tibet to the Arabian Sea and from the Khyber Pass almost to Simla. And when he died the empire went with him. It was a wholly personal achievement but it showed the Sikhs of what they were capable and left them with an example of heroism more suited to their rumbustuous temperament than that of Gandhi and the heroes of Indian independence. Even the British were filled with admiration and subsequently accorded the Sikhs, along with the Gurkhas, pride of place in the Indian Army.

India's immense armed forces still rely heavily on recruitment in the Punjab but the Sardarji is now well represented elsewhere. His great passion other than fighting is for modern technology. Throughout northern India the buses, trains, planes, taxis and lorries are largely manned by Sikhs. The Sikh farmer, like the Jat, a Hindu caste from which many were converted to Sikhism, knows all about irrigation and high-yield cereal strains. The Punjab has become the wheat bowl of India. Here tractors are common and the granaries so full that in 1972 wheat was deteriorating because of the railways' inability to cope with the distribution of such a vast crop. Farther north in the foothills of the Himalayas the Bhakra Hydro dam, second highest in the world, is largely run by Sikhs and it is Sikhs under a Sikh chief engineer who are cutting through a range of the mountains to link the Beas and Sutlej rivers by two vast underground tunnels. Even the doe-eyed teenager tinkering with a motor bike is not, in spite of a ribbon in the hair, a ravishingly pretty Gigi, but a Sardarji schoolboy.

The long hair and strikingly good looks account for endless suspicions of homosexuality. All Indian youths are liable to walk about holding hands and by Western standards even the respectable businessman goes in for a bit too much back-slapping and pawing. My wife insists that much as she appreciates all India's menfolk only the Sardarji does she find attractive. This says much for their masculinity. The Sikhs are probably no more inclined to homosexuality than anyone else; in India it is, anyway, extremely rare. The Sikhs have more of a problem with cigarettes and alcohol. Both are specifically forbidden them but whereas the innocent offer of a cigarette may strike your Sardarji travel agent as a calculated insult, the invitation to a beer will usually be regarded as most acceptable. Like the Rajputs, another warrior people, the Sikhs enjoy a reputation as great drinkers. This may account for the *parvenu*, boorish and almost simple-minded personality attributed them by the more subtle Brahmin. In every Indian equivalent of the Englishman, Scotsman, Irishman joke the Sardarji comes off worst. He is a good enough fellow, a wizard with engines but definitely a little slow and none too sensitive.

At Trichy station in the deep South a neatly dressed Sikh strode rather self-consciously into the non-vegetarian restaurant and in English ordered a chicken curry. I could see the Tamil waiters enjoying a few jokes at his expense and began to feel a great sense of comradeship for him. He was as much a stranger as we were. He flicked open a new black brief case and pulled out a thin notebook and an order pad which he studied with affected seriousness. A new ballpoint emerged from his breast pocket every now and then and I recognised so poignantly that desire to seem at home and relaxed in surroundings totally unfamiliar where, in honesty, one felt just lonely. Probably he was a sales representative;

the technique of selling is as much a part of the new technology as internal combustion. I could imagine him dreaming of the annual conference back in Delhi where over a few bottles of Golden Eagle beer at the President he could tell the latest jokes from the *Readers Digest*'s Humour in Uniform and feel genuinely relaxed and at home.

Surrounded by fellow Sardarji salesmen he would no doubt revert to the usual Sikh banter about how they were financing the country, feeding its people, leading its army and so on. Who but a Sardarji like Swaran Singh could be entrusted with the country's foreign policy and who if not Kushwant Singh★ was the greatest Indian novelist? Considering their numbers the Sikh contribution to modern India is indeed remarkable though the endless boasting is hardly calculated to improve their reputation.

Though greatly influenced by Western ideas they are in many ways the prototype of an Indian community. The Sardarji has his homeland, Punjab, his religion, Sikhism, and his language, Punjabi. He has a group history with its hour of glory, the Sikh empire, and a great leader, Ranjit Singh. To this day his way of life is distinct. 'Sat Sri Akal' rather than 'Namaste' or 'Salaam Aleikum'† is the Sikh greeting. His place of worship is not the temple or the mosque but the 'gurdwara' and his national holy day not Divali or Id but the birthday of Guru Nanak. Not only is the individual Sikh easily identified but the community as a whole has a strong group identity which asserts itself through democratic procedures. Inspired by their history Sikh leaders occasionally raise the cry for Sikh autonomy but so far there has been no need to press the point. They have had their own way with the central government on most issues. The reorganisation of the Punjab‡ in 1956 gave them their own state under the guise of a linguistic award. India's slice of the old Punjab was divided

★ Author of *I Shall Not Hear the Nightingale* and *Train to Pakistan* as well as works on the Sikhs and a biography of Ranjit Singh.

† *Namaste* or *Namaskar* is the Hindu greeting, *Salaam* or *Salaam Aleikum*, the Muslim.

‡ By *the* Punjab I mean the geographical area stretching from the Sutlej to the Indus which, before partition, constituted the province of that name. By Punjab, without the definite article, I mean the state of that name now in the Indian Union.

into two states, Punjab and Haryana. The former includes all Punjabi-speaking areas, that is Sikh areas, the latter all non-Punjabi speaking, that is Hindu, areas. Sikh pressure-groups operate within the Congress Party and outside it through the Akali Party. The latter's success at the polls in 1966 enabled them to win the battle over Chandigarh, capital of the old Punjab state and famous as the work of Le Corbusier. For ten years it had been in dispute between the two new states.

Though Chandigarh is their capital, and Amritsar their Holy City, Delhi may now claim to be the Sikh metropolis. Prior to 1947 Lahore, an ancient Moghul city and subsequently Ranjit Singh's centre of power, had a vast Sikh population. With the creation of Pakistan this city and the western half of the British province of Punjab were severed from India. Communal terror spread on both sides of the new frontier and perhaps the greatest massacre in history accompanied the equally phenomenal exodus of Muslims from the east and Hindus, mostly Sikhs, from the west. A few Sikhs managed to escape from Pakistan to Britain and East Africa but most took refuge in India, particularly in the booming city of Delhi. In Lahore and the surrounding countryside there is now hardly a Sikh to be seen, whilst in Delhi the visitor can be excused for assuming that a good half of India's population is Sikh.

This impression is heightened by the fact that besides his involvement in transport and tourism the Sardarji has no taboos on eating meat provided it is not beef. In all the restaurants and hotels favoured by visitors to Delhi he is very much at home and something of a gourmet where Indian food is concerned. Punjabi cuisine, or the nearest to it that an expatriate East Bengali restaurateur can get, is what passes for Indian food in Indo-Pak restaurants throughout the world. All those tandoori baked chickens, rich mutton curries and substantial nan or chapatti breads are much to the Sardarji's taste though far from representative of Indian cooking as a whole.

★    ★    ★

The Sikh's prowess as a soldier is matched by that of the Muslim Punjabis across the frontier in Pakistan and of the Hindu Punjabis and Jats in what is nowthe Indian state of Haryana. The Punjab, now famous for cereal production, was traditionally a not especially fertile area; its distinction was as India's battlefield. Here in the flat plains to the north and east of Delhi the history of northern India was largely determined. Three decisive battles were fought at Panipat on the main road running north from the city. At near-by Kurukshetra the first great battle of Hindu tradition recorded in the Sanskrit classic, the Mahabharata, took place. Alexander the Great defeated the Indian, Porus, a little to the west on the banks of the Jhelum and even in 1971 the tanks and artillery were again in action between Lahore and Amritsar.

A full account of India's history is beyond the scope of this book. Such a chronicle is, anyway, extremely difficult to compile. Soon after A.D. 1000 most of India was invaded and then conquered by Mohammedan princes from the west. Before this date there is evidence of great civilisations, of invasions and empires spread over three thousand years, yet we know extremely little about them. After the Muslim invasions the succession of events is less conjectural but still the sources are largely non-Indian. Instead of the glimpses afforded by archaeology and the odd traveller's journal we have Muslim chroniclers anxious to chart the victories of Islam. But of Hindu historians there are practically none and it is thus generally assumed that the records scarcely do justice to the majority of Indian people.

In an attempt to fill in the gaps and redress the balance, British and Indian historians have produced two totally different treatments. By way of a rationale for the expansion of their rule the British view of Indian history was that of a naturally lethargic, pacific and disunited jumble of peoples being repeatedly overrun and exploited by more virile outsiders from the north and west. The chronicle is one of repeated invasions, Aryan, Greek, Scythian, Hun, Muslim, Mongol, Persian and British, and the scene is inevitably the Punjab. The pre-Muslim period is treated in the most cursory fashion, little attention being paid to the long periods between invasions and the indigenous kingdoms which arose then. But familiar with the mosques and palaces of Delhi and Agra they studied the Muslim period in detail and traced its later decline towards anarchy thus justifying the imposition of the *Pax Britannica*.

Writing in the context of the struggle for independence, Indian historians regard the later period including that of British rule as the Dark Ages. Emphasis is placed on the religious and cultural integrity of the whole subcontinent in the pre-Muslim period and on the national genius for synthesis and absorption both of indigenous and invading peoples. Nehru took as his premise 'Some kind of dream of unity has occupied the mind of India since the dawn of civilisation'.* In the pre-Muslim period all available evidence is mustered to prove the brilliance and extent of the Mauryan (324–184 B.C.) and Gupta empires (A.D. 320–c. 500). Pride of place goes to those who tried to unite the subcontinent, the mythical Vikram, Chandragupta and Ashoka of the Mauryans, and even the more Indianised Muslims like Ala-ud-din and Tughlaq or, later still, Akbar (1556–1605). A tradition of nationalism is also traced both in the resistance shown to outsiders—Alexander for instance turned back not because his army thought they had marched far enough but because he realised that the opposition was too formidable—and in a thread of revolt lasting through the bleak years of Muslim and British rule; Rajputs, the kingdom of Vijayanagar, Mahrattas, Sikhs and finally the Congress Party all belong to this tradition.

Finally the Indian treatment emphasises the undercurrent of continuity in religious, cultural and social life which no amount of foreign domination was able to destroy. At Harappa in the Punjab and Mohenjo-daro in Sind Indian history begins. The date is perhaps 2000 B.C. Stonehenge may not yet be built. But the remains are not of cave paintings and standing stones but of cities, superbly planned and constructed, with more public amenities and better drainage than their modern counterparts. The history of India is not a progress from barbarism to civilisation. It would appear to

* In his book *Discovery of India*.

have been reasonably civilised for as long as we can trace it. And if there has been little progress there has certainly been continuity. The Indian writer points to the sporadic assertion of traditional values always guarded in the bosom of Indian society but bursting forth to inspire Buddhism and Jainism or the cultural achievements of the Gupta empire.

Whatever the merits of these two views of Indian history it is the latter which is now accepted in India. The new hotels are named after Ashoka or Akbar. Ashoka did all that the Indian historian could wish. His empire extended to the whole subcontinent except the extreme south. He was a veritable Constantine in that he adopted a new religion, Buddhism, but he still insisted on a tolerant treatment of traditional beliefs. Finally, after a bloody conquest of Orissa, he abjured warfare in the best Gandhian tradition of non-violence and outright renunciation. Akbar was never averse to a bit of indiscriminate slaughter but he too united most of the country and followed in the philosopher-king tradition debating with Christians, Hindus and Parsis and urging a very un-Islamic tolerance of his Hindu subjects. The popular heroes of the Independence era are those who resisted the Muslim and British rulers: Prithviraj and the Rajput heroes, Sivaji and the Mahrattas, Ranjit Singh and the Sikhs and, of course, Gandhi, Nehru and Bose. Of the invaders like Alexander the Great, Mahmud of Ghazni (the first Muslim invader), Timur the Lame (the Mongol), the Persian Nadir Shah or Robert Clive little is heard. Even the name of the country on Indian maps is not the British 'India' or the Muslim 'Hindustan' but 'Bharat', a Sanskrit name derived from a mythical founder of the Indo–Aryan people. The idea is to emphasise that the unity of modern India, along with its declared policy of secularism—i.e. no divisive religious discrimination—is not something inherited from the conquering Muslims and British but stems from a purely Indian tradition of homogeneity reaching as far back as history.

Nevertheless, there is no getting away from the extraordinary diversity of India. The constitution adopted at Independence makes this the largest democracy in the world. In Delhi the two houses of parliament operate in true Westernised style but in every state capital there is another assembly legislating according to the American pattern on important local affairs like agriculture, education, health and a variety of taxes. What happens in Chandigarh is likely to hit the Punjabi Sikh harder than what happens in Delhi. The central government can declare the maximum acreage which in socialist India any farmer may own but if Punjab's government is heavily committed to the landed interests it could, and was, dragging its feet interminably on doing anything about it. The whole of India is divided into some twenty such states on the basis of the predominant languages in each area. Some of these states, though occasionally subject to some remote empire in Delhi, have a far longer history as self-governing entities. Gujerat though repeatedly invaded was independent until Akbar's time. Assam successfully resisted all invaders until the nineteenth century. Some of the Rajput states now incorporated in Rajasthan held out through the long years of Muslim rule and were duly recognised as independent princely states by the British.

In many ways the creation of a strong central government has promoted an upsurge of religious pride and a still greater insistence on local and federal traditions. Punjab is not just a Punjabi-speaking state but a Sikh state whilst Kashmir is a predominantly Muslim state. On a Punjab Roadways bus you do not risk lighting a cigarette even if the no-smoking sign is in Punjabi. The Sardarjis would be more than upset. In Kashmir the shops are shut, not on Sundays as elsewhere in India, but on Fridays, the Muslim day of prayer. In the South an innocent inquiry from your Hindi phrasebook will be ignored even by those who know the language. Tamil or English are far more acceptable. But in the North the opposite applies. In 1966 a car in Uttar Pradesh or even Delhi was likely to be stoned if the number plate bore anything except Hindi characters. Language and religion, the two most basic aspects of diversity, matter enormously. But so equally do those of race, caste and politics. As one travels round India one is nagged by a growing suspicion that perhaps the Raj historians were right and that Nehru's dream of unity was, and still is, no more than a dream.

This is reason enough for savouring those first few days in Delhi. For the unity of India is not in race, religion and so on but in a unique way of life. It's in that smell that hits you as you leave the jet, in the crowd that horrifies by its uniformity and confusion and in what I heard a grubby hippie loudly denouncing as the 'shitting and spitting'. Perhaps it's even in what one takes for poverty, the simplicity of dress, food and home.

Delhi, too, reminds one that this unity is a political reality and that this city is the capital, in spite of its vast Sikh community, of a nation of six hundred million of whom the Sikhs are only two per cent. The showpiece of New Delhi, that part of the city built by the British, is a ceremonial way called the Rajpath. Longer and far grander than the Mall, it sweeps down from Raisina Hill and the Rashtrapati Bhawan (once Viceroy's now President's Palace) between the giant Secretariat buildings looking like a set for a Hollywood epic, through and round the imposing India Gate Memorial, past a domed plinth which once sheltered the King Emperor's statue and on to an abrupt stop by a huddle of undistinguished buildings housing a sports stadium. The stadium is, of course, what guide books call 'a subsequent addition'. The idea of the original alignment was to ensure a clear vista to the great shell of the Purana Qila ('ancient fort') beyond— a reminder perhaps to the men of Raisina Hill that they were not the first. Purana Qila is one of a mass of forts, palaces and tombs scattered through the south Delhi suburbs and each testifying to an older empire or a greater sovereign. How many cities have risen and fallen on this site beside the Jumna is anyone's guess. The air-conditioned, tinted glass buses which take you sightseeing stop, and that briefly, at only the most illustrious. But that crumbling domed tomb in the middle of a roundabout which the guide cannot even identify is one of thousands. It's not so much smaller than the Taj Mahal; probably some long-forgotten wife of a great Moghul is buried there. Now, for company, she has a poor outcaste family. The entrance is draped with sacking until the Ancient Monuments people get around to an eviction order.

Of India's four major cities only Delhi has any claim to historical continuity or to responsibilities wider than the purely regional. If the history of India has been determined in the Punjab it has been as often immortalised in Delhi. For both the social and historical perspective it is worth lingering a while before taking a plunge into the crowded bazaars or dashing off into the heart of the subcontinent.

## 2. IMPERIAL LEGACIES

---

# *The North (1)*

When Indians speak of 'The North' they mean not Kashmir and the Himalayas or even the Punjab but rather the Ganges basin, a vast wedge of none-too-exciting country between the Punjab and Bengal. Here in the present-day states of Uttar Pradesh (U.P.) and Bihar live one sixth of the country's total population. Their language, Hindi, is understood by more Indians than any of the country's thirteen other major tongues. Their heritage is the most respected in India. Here the Indo–Aryans, equivalent to the Anglo–Saxons as the ancestral race from whom the nation likes to trace its genius, put down their roots in the rich alluvial soil. This was the setting for the classics of Sanskrit literature from which Hinduism derives and subsequently the cradle of Buddhism and Jainism, the two great reform movements of the sixth century B.C. For Ashoka and the rulers of the Mauryan and Gupta kingdoms the North was the seat of empire just as centuries later it was to be the core first of Muslim and then of British rule. Not surprisingly the people of the North regard their homeland as India itself and the rest of the subcontinent as little more than a colonial appendage.

Looking at the Gangetic plain today it is hard to believe that this tired, dusty and monotonous land could have been the prize that drew wave upon wave of invaders down the Khyber Pass and across the Punjab or which supported the magnificence of empires and yielded unique cultural flowerings. As late as March the papers in 1972 were full of 'more cold deaths in Bihar' then, just two months later, it was 'heat wave toll rises, 118° F in Bihar'. Besides the extremes of temperature the whole area is renowned for its monsoon floods, its famines and, above all, its poverty.

There are sizeable cities like Lucknow, Benares, Allahabad, there are industrial complexes at Barauni and Kanpur (Cawnpore) and there are as always in India a few wealthy land-owning families. But the North, *par excellence*, is the land of the rural poor.

For no apparent reason the train slows to a halt in the middle of nowhere. You suddenly become conscious of the searing, glaring heat and rashly open the window. It is as hot and breathless as it looks but what hits you first is the silence. A vast, pale, pulsating sky, a stretch of shimmering flat soil relieved by the odd patch of something green and this total, terrifying silence. The silence, in fact, of the desert. Yet deserted it certainly isn't. Though wood for burning is as scarce as stone for building this is one of Asia's more closely populated areas. From the patch of green comes a shout; people begin to appear from nowhere out of the flat soil. And from the village you had not even noticed, so well do its mud huts blend with the earth on which it stands, there emerges a distant figure tearing across the fields with a whole branch of bananas. He hopes to sell them to the train's passengers. An ox-cart has appeared on the horizon. You can hear it creaking, a sound so familiar to the men in the fields that they scarcely notice it but, like the smells, so typically Indian and, to those who love India, so very evocative. I should hate to be thought guilty of romanticising poverty but there is about the rural poverty of India great beauty as well as sadness. The little group of figures standing in the field, looking anxiously from the train to the branch of bananas dancing towards them, may be thin but they have a grace, an erectness and a physique more proud and infinitely more beautiful than any navvy or longshoreman. The train gives a lurch and begins to crawl forward, the passengers who had got out for a stretch clamber back aboard and for a minute the running figure with the bananas continues to gain ground. But he is too late. The signal must have changed. The train is picking up speed and already the silence, like the dust, is beginning to settle on the endless flat earth behind, on the dispersing labourers and on the tired banana runner.

Eighty per cent of India's population live in villages and seventy-

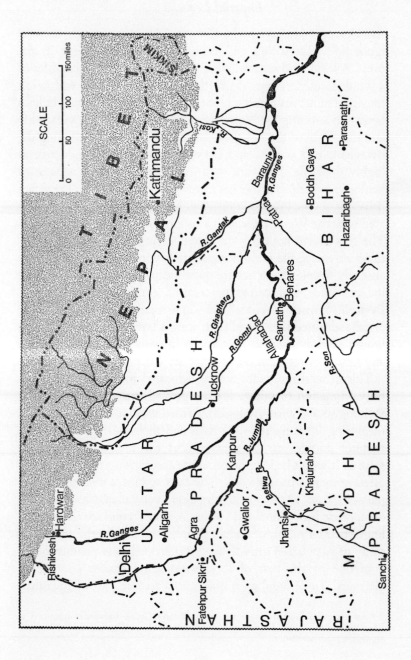

five per cent are said to be illiterate. Alarming stories of rural ignorance, superstition and brutality frequently appear in the press. A local feud somewhere in Orissa results in the slaughter of a whole family. A case of *sati* (the ritual burning of a widow on the death of her husband) is reported from Bihar. Educated Indians betray an amazing ignorance, often indifference, about village life and the plight of the villagers. To the Hindu way of thinking the ownership of a plot of land, however small and unproductive, is highly desirable. Everyone you meet seems to have a piece of land somewhere. But this has never produced amongst the richer urban classes the love and understanding of the countryside associated with the Western ideals of a country seat or weekend cottage. The few Indian novelists who have attempted to portray something of village life seldom penetrate beyond the exteriors. Their absurdly simple characters are quite incapable of the violence and independence attributed to their real-life equivalents by the press.*
Even G., himself a writer living in a small market town in the South, admitted that the villages were a law unto themselves. He would need to spend at least a year in even a local village to get any idea of what went on or what the villagers thought.

This general ignorance among educated Indians and the continued isolation of village life has proved irresistible to Western sociologists and anthropologists. Armed with questionnaires, head measuring instruments, slide rules and theories they descend on remoter corners of the subcontinent for the winter 'research season'. It won't be long before some enterprising travel agency is offering them a package deal. The caste system, a uniquely Indian phenomenon, is the great attraction, particularly its effect on democratic procedures and voting. A close second are the origins, linguistic and racial, of India's peoples and finally the inevitable study of population growth against increased food production.

In one of the best of these sociological studies (G. Morris Carstairs' *Twice Born*) an old man in a remote part of Rajasthan

---

* An exception must be made for Prem Chand's *Godan*, sometimes translated as *The Gift of a Cow*. His villagers go to the other extreme. They are too violent and obstinate to be credible.

is quoted as asking whether it was true that the British had left Delhi. They had; this was 1963. 'Then I imagine the Moghuls are back.'

Isolated, illiterate and largely ignored I suppose it is conceivable that the Indian villager should repay indifference with indifference on this scale. But this largely illiterate eighty per cent of the population has roused itself six or seven times in the last twenty-five years to walk up to two miles* to the polling booths and in the most responsible fashion to elect a national government. Always there is talk of bought votes, of rigged registers, of Untouchables being turned away and of lost ballot boxes. It is assumed that most rural voters will put their mark wherever caste or religious leaders tell them and that official transport will be commandeered for ferrying voters by those already in power. Yet somehow elections in India work. The total vote usually amounts to nearly sixty per cent of the electorate—a creditable figure in a predominantly rural society.

In view of the size of its population nowhere is the vote more decisive than in the Ganges plain. Significantly India's three Prime Ministers, Jawaharlal Nehru, Lal Bahadur Shastri and Indira Gandhi, have all been elected from U.P. constituencies. Door-to-door canvassing in constituencies averaging half a million voters is clearly impractical but the dust churned up by party workers on bicycles, ox-carts and jeeps during the run up to the polls is testimony enough to a real effort to present the issues to the people. It's those men in the field, not the man in the street, who decide the outcome of an election. And if through twenty-five years they have remained predominantly loyal to one party, the Congress, it is not purely out of ignorance of an alternative.

During this period rural life in India has undergone more change than in the whole of its unwritten history. Certainly affluence is still remote but in the changeless context of village society even the arrival of those awful plastic shoes is something of a revolution. Most villages now have their own, or access to, a

---

* Polling booths were supposed to be a maximum of two miles, now reduced to one and a half, from any village. Often they are nearer, sometimes considerably farther.

primary school. They have a village dispensary decorated with family planning posters and a bus which once a day appears in a cloud of dust and disappears with more dust towards the nearest market town. The tea shop may well boast a radio. It makes one nostalgic for the frightening silence but it means that even the illiterate can keep abreast with events and current movie themes. In the more prosperous villages of Punjab and western U.P. bicycles are a common sight and as always the trains everywhere are overflowing with villagers. The tube-well, after years of nothing but promises, materialised rather rapidly just before the last election. Villagers accused of having sold their votes for it are unimpressed. After all if democracy brings progress why complain? The population figures continue to soar but if family planning has not yet caught on, the use of high-yield cereals and of irrigation is fully appreciated. Early in 1972 when further food imports from the U.S.A. were stopped it was announced that, given an average monsoon, the country was at last self-sufficient in basic foodstuffs. Without reference to any statistics I can confirm that as against the situation even six years ago the Gangetic plain looks considerably greener and less desperate.

The burden of poverty is not wholly insupportable when you have enough to eat and everyone around you is living at much the same level. Sleeping along with your friends in the streets of Bombay where the temperature rarely falls below 70° F is a lot more comfortable and enjoyable than the sort of night Orwell's Clergyman's Daughter spent in Trafalgar Square in November. And being without enough possessions to fill a suitcase or enough money to buy a bus ticket is not quite so bad in an Indian village as in New York. One must be careful not to pity the simplicity of the village home. Simple food, lack of furniture, simple clothing and a minute room or house are actually preferred by many. Poverty is to be witnessed not so much in how people live as in how they celebrate. The winter, which is the tourist season, is also the wedding season. A man is to be pitied when the best he can afford for his daughter's wedding includes neither a band nor massive candelabra. Or when instead of the traditional white horse for the groom, he arrives walking with a cardboard cut-out of a horse strapped between his thighs.

For all rural communities life is perilous; a poor monsoon or a heavy monsoon, a credit squeeze by the ubiquitous money-lenders or, for cash crop producers, a drop in world prices may mean starvation in a matter of weeks. In 1972 the Gangetic plain was not seriously beset by any of these things. However bad the position in Western India a succession of good harvests had reminded people that this alluvial soil washed down from the Himalayas is some of the richest in the world. It could be another wheat bowl like the prairies but with a second harvest each year, just as productive, of pulses and sugar cane. Mrs. Gandhi's election slogan, 'Gharibi hatao' (Do away with poverty) though not very original, could yet have substance.

*    *    *

Prominent amongst the rural poor, particularly in the North, are India's Muslims.* They constitute more than thirty per cent of the population in many parts of U.P. and Bihar. The visitor seldom comes into any social contact with them but reminders of this considerable slice of the population are everywhere. Delhi is full of colossal red sandstone tombs, palaces and mosques from the heyday of Islamic power. So, too, is Agra, the first step on what the tour operators call 'the milk run', a two-day jaunt round the sights of the Gangetic plain. Most famous of all these monuments is the Taj Mahal, another tomb but this time built out of sumptuous white marble. After a glut of buildings fashioned out of chunks of dull salmon stone generations of tourists must have heaved a sigh of relief on seeing the opaque brilliance of its handsome dome.

This seemed reason enough for its fame, added to the fact that Agra is a convenient distance from Delhi. You can fly, go by train or drive there and back in a day. And every day thousands do. Had the emperor Shah Jehan, buried his beloved wife Mumtaz

---

* Mohammedans are known as Muslims or Moslems throughout the East.

Mahal at Burhanpur in the Deccan where she actually died it might have been a very different story. So, at least, I felt before actually joining the crowds for a trip to Agra. Universal acclaim had made of my initial reservations a real barrage of sceptical objections; I knew I wouldn't like it but at least I was not going to be disappointed. Cautiously I peeped round the side of the gateway, another colossus in red sandstone. It was dark and deep but framed in the archway and etched against a deep blue sky rode this dazzling image of light. I suppose it was inevitable. My reservations were swept under, dashed to pieces and forgotten— a total catharsis.

My wife is less cautious and more open. On a subsequent occasion I was as interested to see her reactions as to see the Taj. By taking a circuitous route and distracting her attention every time the great white dome could be seen floating like a cloud above the tree tops we had reached that same gateway without her appetite being spoilt by any premature glimpses. The Taj Mahal is more of a happening, a total experience, than just a building. Hidden by large trees and a walled garden it relies heavily on its initial impact and its superb position with just the sky for a back drop. You enter the garden, as a church, from the back. The formal flower-beds with paths and water course form a straight nave flanked by tall trees leading the eye to the great raised marble sanctuary on which sits, or floats, this most perfect of buildings, part stone, part sky. It was a Friday and this being, as well as a national institution a Muslim shrine, entrance on the day of prayer was free. In the red sandstone gateway there was a dense crowd, black silk bourkas with heavily barred eyeslits and, inside, orthodox Muslim ladies were blundering about behind a wall of American visitors changing to wide angles for a shot of the Taj framed by the gateway. Amongst them I lost J. When I found her she was standing quietly on one side apparently hypnotised. The only sign of life was a steady trickle of tears down each cheek.

The Taj Mahal is a sad building. Sad because all things of sublime beauty make those painfully aware of their own and the world's imperfections feel sad. Sad because of its romantic associations as the monument to a great love and the tomb of a queen whose king, through years of hardship and imprisonment, never became reconciled to her loss. And now perhaps sad because, beside this product of the greatness and nobility of Islam in India, one must set the plight and degradation of India's sixty million Muslims. Though by far the most numerous of the country's minority groups Nirad Chaudhuri calls them 'the least of the minorities'*—least because their status and influence in post independence society in no way matches their numerical strength. Predominantly they are to be found amongst the rural poor. Throughout U.P. and Bihar there are scattered Muslim villages and in every small town there is a Muslim district. The mosque is a walled enclosure with often a short but intricate minaret and the whole village or district has a noticeably shut-in look. The women are kept out of sight and the houses shuttered. One is reminded of a ghetto but the introspection is as much self-imposed as anything.

The Muslims of India are mostly converts. From A.D. 1001 onwards a succession of Mohammedan invaders penetrated the subcontinent destroying Hindu temples, slaughtering the people and proclaiming the supremacy of Islam. The first waves culminated about A.D. 1200 in the setting up of a kingdom or Sultanate in Delhi. Immediately construction of the colossal mosques and palaces which constitute the historical heritage of the North began. The first was the Qutb Minar and mosque in Delhi. The Sultanate changed hands, under Ala-ud-din and Mohammed Tughlaq its authority reached deep into the Deccan, Gujerat and Bengal and then retracted. But under local Muslim rulers the process of conquest and conversion went on along with the building tradition in the development of the Indo–Saracenic style. The Mongol, Timur the Lame (Tamburlane), invaded the North in 1398 and it was a distant descendant of his, Babur, who in 1526 finally uprooted the Delhi Sultanate and founded the Moghul (i.e. Mongol) empire, the golden age of Islam in India.

★ In his book *The Continent of Circe.*

There were six 'Great Moghuls' covering the period 1526–1707; Babur, the conqueror from Afghanistan, gained a foothold in India. Humayun nearly lost it but boasts the finest of the Moghul tombs bar the Taj.* Akbar, the greatest warrior and the most enlightened ruler, built the city of Fatehpur Sikri. Jehangir was given to excesses of every sort but did Kashmir a great service by patronising it as a resort. Shah Jehan presided over the greatest period of Moghul architecture and besides the Taj Mahal built the Jama Masjid and the Red Fort in Delhi. And finally Aurangzeb, the nigger in the woodpile so far as Indian historians are concerned because his bigotry led to the severe persecution of Hindus. In name the empire staggered on for another one hundred and fifty years, the last emperor being packed off to Burma by the British for his part in the 1857 mutiny.

Throughout these centuries of Muslim rule Hindus, mostly from the lower castes, were finding it easier and cheaper (a poll tax was leved on non-Muslims) to be Muslims, whilst the invading princes were marrying local Hindu princesses, and becoming more and more Indianised. By 1857 and the Indian mutiny the emperor could be regarded as a figurehead not of Moghul oppression but of Indian aspirations. Likewise the converts to Islam regarded themselves not as Muslims by convenience but by tradition. The population was irrevocably divided into two religions.

Under British rule Muslims continued to enjoy preferential treatment, initially in deference to their former status, latterly as a counter-weight to the predominantly Hindu demand for self rule expressed through the Congress Party. Urdu, the language of India's Muslims and now of Pakistan, was accepted by the army as the official native language. On the much-daubed walls of Delhi, Agra and Lucknow its flowing Persian or Arabic script contrasts with the angular Hindi characters strung together as on a washing line. The Muslim's comparative freedom from taboos on eating also recommended him as a domestic servant in European households.

But with Independence and partition everything changed. The

* Humayun's tomb is in south Delhi.

rich and influential, the products of the famous Muslim University at Aligarh, largely opted for Pakistan and moved there. Those who stayed behind were moderates and supporters of the Congress Party. They could never aspire to the mass support given to Jinnah and radical Muslim leaders. In Punjab and Bengal the peasantry followed their leaders but elsewhere India was left with the poorer members, mostly originally converts from the humblest castes, largely rural and uneducated and, worst of all, spread fairly evenly throughout the whole country. Although belonging to the world's second largest Mohammedan community* they naturally feel vulnerable in an overwhelmingly Hindu society. There has been a Muslim President and several Muslim cabinet ministers, the government is for ever emphasising the secular nature of the Constitution and of its own policies, yet a sense of discrimination is still felt by most Muslims. In advocating partition the Muslim leaders of the 1940s must take much of the blame for the plight of India's Muslims today. In their bid for Pakistan, a separate state for those areas of British India with a Muslim majority, they sacrificed the interests of those Muslims who were in a minority status elsewhere. Partition left them leaderless and the mounting animosity between India and Pakistan only emphasised their isolation. The Muslims of India who in a united subcontinent would have been sufficiently strong and influential to safeguard their own interests† are now a suspicious and reticent community who see their chief hope in flouting the family planning advertisements whilst the Hindu majority queue up for sterilisation.

In the vast mosque at Fatehpur Sikri, or that beside the Imam Bara in Lucknow, local Muslims pray and picnic in the shadow of their former greatness. For them the fame of the emperors and the Nawabs‡ is not just part of Indian history. They feel something more like the bitterness and sense of isolation experienced

---

* The largest is that of Indonesia. Asians outnumber Arabs in the world's Muslim population by at least ten to one.

† Before partition the Muslims were a quarter of the population. In India they are now about one-tenth.

‡ Nawabs were the Muslim equivalents of Rajas and Maharajas.

by those British who stayed on in India after 1947 and ruefully observe the removal of the Queen-Empress's statue and the gradual eclipse of the English language. Even though of native origin Indian Muslims are an easily recognised community. On any sizeable station in U.P. or Bihar there will be at least one family of landless Muslim peasants going perhaps on pilgrimage to the great centre of north-Indian Islam at Ajmer. The father has a straggly beard—Hindus, unless they are *Saddhus* or Sikhs, rarely grow one—and wears a black fez of Persian lamb skin. Grandfather has been to Mecca and is a pillar of orthodoxy; his white beard is streaked with henna and he wears a soiled skullcap. The women in the party are sweating in *purdah*, grandmother and grand-daughter indistinguishable beneath their dark *bourkas*, voluminous trousers and satin slippers.

To accusations of discrimination against the Muslims the Hindu may reply that all castes and communities in India suffer from discrimination. The lot of the Muslim is often no worse than that of those to whose caste his family once belonged. Besides, do not Muslims themselves discriminate both against low caste Hindus and other Muslims? For besides being divided into the different Mohammedan sects—Sunni, Shiah and Ismaili—the Indian Muslims have their own parallel caste system. As a community they are as faction-ridden and disunited as the Hindus. In Lucknow during the 1971 elections it was a foregone conclusion that whichever party the Sunnis supported the Shiahs would oppose and that dissenting castes within each sect would likewise adopt an opposition candidate. This sort of attitude explains the enormous number of candidates, usually five to ten, who contest every seat. Mrs. Gandhi and her father were widely credited with having won the Muslim vote in most areas but from this it should never be thought that the Muslims are guarding their interests by a united approach to the polls. In many areas there is a Muslim League party though as often as not its candidate will be a Hindu. The idea is that besides the bulk of the Muslim vote he should attract a few Hindu votes. The Muslim vote is rarely if ever large enough or cohesive enough to ensure a

majority. Opposition parties, even the militant Hindu Jan Sangh
Party, immediately capitalise by themselves putting up a Muslim.
And so for the illiterate Muslim peasant confusion is compounded.

In the sleepy little town of Hazaribagh in Bihar we were watching the preparations for the 1972 state elections. The shops in the
Muslim streets of the bazaar, mostly tailors and cafés, all flew the
gay yellow flag of the Jan Sangh. It made about as much sense as
a Negro vote for Goldwater or Enoch Powell. The Jan Sangh's
avowed aim is to rouse Hindu nationalism but the *mullah* of
Hazaribagh clearly overlooked this in favour of an irresponsible
pledge by the local party leaders to work for the repatriation to
India of fellow Bihari Muslims in the new state of Bangladesh.
With his help the Jan Sangh candidate was duly elected.

\* \* \*

Besides the Muslim legacy of mosques and tombs India boasts
imperial relics of a more utilitarian nature. Ten feet wide by a
good one thousand two hundred miles long a strip of tarmac
threads its way the length of the Gangetic plain from Calcutta to
Delhi and on across the frontier to Lahore and Peshawar. On each
side there is a shoulder of pitted earth exploding into dust during
the dry season and knee deep in mud during the monsoon. Shad-
ing it from the sun and demarcating it from the equally dusty or
muddy fields are two lines of tall trees, shady peepuls, sombre
mangoes, delicate neems or giant banyans writhing with branch-
high roots like Laocoon with the snakes. This is the Grand Trunk
Road, India's Route 66. Thanks to Kipling it conjures up much
that is romantic about India; pilgrims, outlaws, nomads and the
life of the road. Nowadays Kim and the Lama would find it less
congenial. India is thought to have the distinction of, given the
volume of traffic, the highest accident rate in the world. Certainly
the G.T. must rank amongst the most alarming highways. King
of the road is the Punjabi truck-driver. He knows it backwards.
He knows that our car and his lorry cannot pass each other and
both remain on the narrow strip of tarmac. At least one of us

will have to lurch on to the dangerously rutted shoulder. And he knows to a fraction of a second how late he can leave it before one of us must wrench the wheel to the left.★ The smallest errors of judgement are attested, more frequently than petrol stations, in crumpled, suppurating wrecks thrown into the clutches of a banyan or up-ended on the embankment.

'Why do you carry a gun in the glove pocket?'

'Trucks,' yelled K. as he rested an elbow on the horn to inform the one in front of us that he wished to overtake.

'Over-reacting a bit isn't it?'

'Not the driver. Just his tyres. Here.'

I passed the cold weapon over. He leant out of the window to take aim but the truck wisely swung off the tarmac with a screech of brakes.

'Pity,' mumbled K.

Like the railways and the post office, the administrative service, the army, the Survey of India and even the Constitution, the Grand Trunk Road is a legacy of the British. In two hundred years they made a more striking impression than the Muslims in eight hundred. Above all they made a reality of Indian unity where even the Moghuls had failed. They measured and mapped, standardised and centralised, bridged and tunnelled until the whole subcontinent was a workable entity. There was no question of altruism or of realising Nehru's dream of unity for him. Only by thus transforming the country could the British hope to hold it. Colonisation by a massive British migration to India was out of the question. The Indian empire was won by adventurers, secured by engineers and run by a small *élite* of administrators.

It is often said that there are more British in India today than at any time during the Raj. In India, perhaps, but not of India. Typical of them would be the bank clerks and middle grade executives of British companies in Bombay and Calcutta. Their status is little better than that of indentured labourers. Recruited from some dour Scottish insurance office they sign on for thirty

★ Throughout the subcontinent one drives on the left, another British legacy.

months with an undertaking to stay single and avoid all unnecessary contact with Indians. India for them is to mean no more than the Company's balance sheet. Of the British who were associated with the Raj there are few survivors. The odd missionary lady still soldiers on in Kashmir and central India, a few tea planters stayed on in Assam and there's a lonely headmaster or two still character building in India's imitation Etons. Calcutta has a fair number of well established British businessmen or industrialists and in the hill stations one encounters an occasional retired colonel or widow who rejected the allure of Cheltenham. But that's all. As a community they scarcely exist though the imperial tradition they represent is quite as striking in contemporary India as that represented by the sixty million Muslims.

What the British did and did not do for India is an argument which history may never resolve. It was by every account an extraordinary encounter from which neither party has yet recovered. There are the roads and the railways which are so much a part of India today that it seems captious to regard their construction simply as a more effective method of suppressing the Indian people. There are the Lutyens buildings of New Delhi, the Secretariat, Viceroy's Palace and Parliament House, indicative in their very functions of an odd kind of empire that wished to go on governing but only with the co-operation of the Indian people. There is the Higginbotham's bookshop on every station platform in the South testifying to the great cultural exchange between Anglo–Saxon and Indo–Aryan. Or there are the timbered Kingston-by-pass villas of Simla reminding one of the aloofness, the pettiness and the sheer obstinacy of many representatives of the Raj.

All these and many other relics of the Raj have their significance. But there is one event in the two hundred odd years of British rule, one place and one moment, which coloured the whole strange Indo–British relationship. The Indian Mutiny (to Indian historians The National Uprising), Lucknow, 1857.

Lucknow today is not a beautiful city. It sprawls beside the Gomti river in the heart of U.P. There are more cycle rickshaws, more peeling crumbling buildings, more open drains than one finds in most provincial capitals. But in Kim's day it was different. 'No city—except Bombay, the queen of all—(was) more beautiful in her garish style than Lucknow'. It was a city of luxury famous for its silks, perfumes and jewellery. A place, in fact, to fight and die for. So at least thought many of the three thousand who spent the worst of the summer and monsoon of 1857 behind the walls of the British residency compound. They were not most of them born heroes; they were more like something out of a Happy Families pack of British India. There was poor Mr. Polehampton the chaplain, 'who preached a beautiful sermon' and was shot while shaving for Holy Communion. Mr. Gubbins the finance commissioner, Colonel Case the eternal joker 'who always looked on the bright side'—what a bore he must have been—and the plucky Private Cuney who, with his faithful sepoy, specialised, like some renegade fifth-former, in unauthorised night raids on the enemy lines. The besieged held out for nearly four months. As if aware of the siege's potential as a film script they committed suicide, enjoyed love affairs, gave birth, indulged in acts of outrageous valour, contrived some remarkable escapes and got killed. One of the first to go was the British Resident, Sir Henry Lawrence. He was hit on the third day and died in great pain on the fifth. A pot of honey from his kit fetched £4 as prices rose and smallpox, scurvy and cholera set in. Of the three thousand British and Indians who sought refuge in the Residency on June 30th only one thousand marched out on November 18th.

The ruins of the Residency, spattered with memorial plaques like some much decorated Chelsea Pensioner, still stand though the walls and surrounding buildings have been completely demolished. There's an old gentleman, a Muslim, who buttonholes you as you squeeze through a turnstile into the Residency drawing-room, now a museum. In a mechanical voice which is difficult to follow he recites the whole saga of the siege. It takes twenty minutes, brooking no interruptions and one suspects including a few chapters of the Koran when his memory fails; he expects fifty paise but more if you cut him short. He will also show you the whereabouts of Sir Henry Lawrence's grave. A few goats are picking about the cemetery which is more remarkable for the size of the tombstones than their number. Sir Henry's is comparatively modest and the famous inscription only just legible. 'Here lies Henry Lawrence who tried to do his duty. May the Lord have mercy on his soul'.

Just outside the Residency on the banks of the Gomti river an enormous white Cleopatra's needle has been erected to commemorate 'The Nationalist Insurgents' who lost their lives in 1857—a reasonable enough gesture to national pride. One would have expected the architects of Indian Independence to have made a good deal of the nationalist leaders. But not so. The three significant figures on the Indian side, Nana Sahib who claimed to be a Mahratta descendant, Tantia Topi, his best general, and the heroic Princess of Jhansi receive scant acclaim. The Indian historian accords the uprising national status, yet dismisses its leaders as feudal reactionaries concerned not with the united, independent India of the future but hopeful simply of restoring the old order of aggressive local states. British historians tend to emphasise that it was not even a national affair. It was just an army mutiny without civilian support and was restricted purely to the Bengal Presidency, which in those days covered the whole of the North. Even within this narrow definition it was not unanimously supported. About half of those defending the Lucknow residency were Indian soldiers.

Why was it then in any way significant and why on earth is it called the Indian Mutiny or the Nationalist Uprising? An explanation might be found not in its causes but its results. The British promptly removed the last Moghul, ended the days of the East India Company in favour of direct rule by the Crown, reorganised the administration and started building railways in earnest. Had there been a line through the Gangetic plain the Memsahibs at Lucknow, Kanpur and Delhi could have been evacuated and loyal troops rushed up to help the besieged garrisons. In short the British got a fright from which they never completely recovered. 'The Mutiny' was never forgotten. It failed but had it really been a national uprising it would surely have succeeded. The possibility of such a disaster was enough to ensure that once the demand for independence became widespread no British government could ignore or resist it.

To the Indian people it demonstrated the precarious nature of British empire and established that not violence but unity and cohesion would be sufficient to supplant it. Eight hundred years of Muslim rule had added a new tear to the already perished fabric of Indian society. Whatever its intended policy British rule and particularly the lesson of 1857 had the opposite effect. A nation could be at least partly knitted together in the knowledge that the Raj was not invincible. The British, unlike the Muslim powers or anyone else who had settled in India, saw themselves as one people, one nation. Why not the Indians too? The Muslim–Hindu rift was never bridged but to judge by Mahatma Gandhi's attempts to unite Indians of every caste and religion the point was well taken.

## *The North (2)*

The Indian historian can afford to dismiss nine hundred years of
British and Muslim rule as a sort of dark ages because before that,
before A.D. 1000, there lie two or three thousand years of vague
but distinguished Indian history. With this period the two great
cities of the eastern end of the northern plain, Patna and Benares,
are particularly associated. The region is the heartland of the
Indo–Aryans, India's predominant ethnic group, and through it
winds the Ganges, the holy river of the Hindus; both Patna and
Benares lie beside it. The period includes the classical age of
Indian culture and, like the Ganges, there flows through it a
developing religious tradition which we know as Hinduism and
which to most Indians represents the genius of the nation.

Patna, an even more unlovely city than Lucknow, was once
the magnificent Pataliputra, capital of the Magadha kingdom and
seat of both the Mauryan and Gupta empires. Making free with
history one could compare these with the Greek and Roman
empires. Both occurred about two hundred years later than their
Mediterranean counterparts but both occasioned a succession of
illustrious rulers commanding a vast empire, a brilliant court and
a great cultural and religious upsurge. Megasthenes, a Greek
ambassador to the court of the first Mauryan (c. 300 B.C.) paints a
portrait of the life and times there which is recognisably Indian
even by today's standards.

Sources for the period are extremely scarce. Apart from Megasthenes, information about the Mauryans is chiefly gleaned from
the inscriptions of the third emperor, Ashoka. Predictably he
emerges with an exceptionally good press. Ashoka's authority
extended to the whole subcontinent except the extreme south;

he established himself as a merciless conqueror but then forswore warfare and concentrated on the physical and moral uplift of his subjects. The squiggly writing of the inscriptions on the pillars at Sarnath, Sanchi, Allahabad and Delhi and on rocks scattered throughout his empire tell his subjects to respect life, to be tolerant of sectarianism, to speak the truth, love their relatives and live righteous lives. Ashoka was greatly influenced by Buddhist teaching and was himself a lay brother. Buddhism was a sect or cult within the religious life of the country. Although critical of Brahmin traditions and teachings it was never regarded as an alternative religion; it was part of the developing religious life of the subcontinent and as such its teachings were progressively reabsorbed into the Hindu tradition.

Ashoka's pillars are famous for their message rather than their shape. If the Mauryan contribution to the civilisation of classical India was moral and religious that of the Guptas was cultural and artistic. In the period between the two empires great progress was made in sculpture and architecture as witnessed by the *stupas*, Buddhist tombs, at Sarnath and Sanchi. By A.D. 320, the beginning of the Gupta era, the first caves had been cut at Ajanta and Ellora and craftsmen were ready to tackle the statuary, pillars and domes of the finest caves at both these sites as well as Elephanta and Kanheri near Bombay. Typical of the Gupta emperors was Samudragupta I (c. A.D. 335–385) who besides vast conquests in central, eastern and western India was an accomplished administrator, poet and musician. This was the great age of Sanskrit, the classical language of India. Kalidasa, the most famous name in Indian letters attended the court of Samudragupta's successor. Kautilya, the Indian Macchiavelli, compiled his Arthasastra on the art of government whilst the Kamasutra, another social compendium, was being put together by Vatsyayana.

At Patna the remains of the imperial city are disappointing. Then as now stone was scarce in the Gangetic plain. The city was built largely of wood. This explains why the great monuments of the period are not in U.P. and Bihar but far away in the Vindhya Hills and Maharashtra. On the other hand the distribution of the caves and temples or the *stupas*, rock edicts and pillars of the Mauryas gives some idea of the extent of these empires. They were as pan-Indian as, much later, those of the Moghuls and British. Political unity was not the invention of foreign rulers.

Equally a part of Indian tradition are the Buddhist and Jain contributions to this cultural flowering. Ashoka was a Buddhist, the Guptas were Hindus and most of the cave temples were Jain or Buddhist. Yet each was a part of the same religious tradition. Ashoka preached respect for Brahmins and today Jain and Buddhist ethics are an essential part of Hinduism. There was no sense of opposing religions or divergent trends. A little south from Patna lies Boddh Gaya, scene of the Buddha's enlightenment. Buddhists come here from all over the Far East yet they seldom outnumber the devotees of Siva and Vishnu for whom the place is just as hallowed.

More significant for Hinduism today yet older still than Pataliputra is the ancient city of Kasi. Indian Railways run a train called the Kasi Express, Indian Airlines insist on calling the city Varanasi but for most people it is still Benares, the sacred city of the Hindus, as hallowed as Mecca but like Hinduism itself a good deal less exclusive. A pilgrimage to the city's temples, a drink of the Ganges water or a bathe in the sacred river here qualifies as a plenary indulgence. All sin, all failings in pursuit of *dharma*, are forgiven. And of course to die here is a surefire way of achieving paradise, release from the cycle of rebirth into the oblivion of *moksha*, the Hindu *nirvana*.

'Sahib, this my cycle of rebirth, I take you bathing ghats.'* It was 6.00 a.m., the rush hour for sightseers. We squeezed into a dewy rickshaw and set off for the Ganges. The better hotels in Benares as in most Indian cities are located in something called 'The Cantonment'. This is not as one fears a barbed-wire enclosure full of soldiers but a peaceful residential area with large houses in big gardens. Here the sahibs could escape from India to a mock

* In this case steps leading down to the river but, more generally, any steep embankment or hillside. Hence the Eastern and Western Ghats, the coastal mountains of the peninsula.

Chesham Bois and concentrate on bridge and growing dahlias. Once outside the cantonment we were rattling down a street lined with shoemakers' shops; working in leather, the skin of the sacred cow, is a detestable pursuit which relegates the cobbler to the lowest of castes. There is always a suspicion that he may in acquiring the skin be tempted to taste the forbidden flesh. After them come the wood choppers. In Benares chopping wood is a major industry. Thousands of bodies must be cremated every day and the municipal authorities are liable to make big trouble if through economising on the pyre a charred limb should be left to litter the river bank. In itself there is nothing wrong in chopping wood but in view of its particular connotation here the wood choppers, like the cobblers and the sahibs, are located well away from the holy bathing ghats and the bazaars.

We rattled on, part of a growing surge of people and vehicles heading for the river bank. I was thinking about Hinduism and wondering how on earth one could begin to explain what it is all about. Something that Arthur Koestler* wrote will help as a preliminary—'The attempt to translate it into the verbal concepts and categorical structure of Western language leads to logical monstrosities.' In Eastern philosophies symbolic and literal meanings were never separated; concepts and grammar remained fluid. To many Indians it is this very lack of definition in belief which is so appealing. There are no Aristotles nor St. Pauls in Hindu tradition and theology never fell a prey to the bloodless reasoning of an Aquinas. Quite the opposite. It went in for great woolly visions of life and a profuse assortment of jolly, voluptuous and sometimes frightening deities.

Hinduism is not a religion in the sense that Christianity or Islam is. 'Hindu' and 'India' both come from the same root—'Indus', people *of* the Indus or *beyond* the Indus. Before the Mohammedans arrived there was no call for distinguishing between the Hindus and Indians. They were the same thing. Even Buddhists were Hindus. As with the Jews if you were born of Indian parents you were an Indian, i.e. a Hindu. Nowadays writers on Indian religion

* In *Lotus and the Robot*.

seldom talk of Hinduism. Instead they have parcelled the whole thing out into Vedism, Brahmanism, Saivism, Vaisnavism, neo-syncretism, etc.,* hoping thus to eliminate some of the contradictions and so reduce it to doctrinal packages of a manageable size. This is all very well for students of comparative religions but it does not help to understand what is going on in Benares. Ask an Indian if he is a Vedist and he will, if he understands what you are on about, say yes. A Brahmanist? Yes. Saivite? Yes. And so on. Probably if you asked him if he believed in Jesus Christ and Jupiter he would also say yes. It is not just that he does not wish to disappoint you. He knows nothing of a bar on false gods and graven images; the more the better. How wrong it would be to deny a god, a body of doctrine, that might exist and be true.

What passes for the earliest history of India, before about 500 B.C., is the history of what I will continue to call Hinduism. Over a number of centuries at the beginning of the second millennium B.C. a pastoral race known as the Aryans poured into northern India as they did into Europe. They spoke a language or something very like it called Sanskrit and they were taller and fairer than the people already in India. I have sat in a railway carriage on the Punjab Mail opposite an elderly couple whose resemblance to my grandparents was uncanny. In old people the skin grows pale and composes itself about the bone structure in a way that emphasises the features. European or Indian, the Aryan in us all becomes unmistakable. These Aryan invaders brought with them an oral tradition of prayers and sacrificial directives known as the Vedas. They were duly recorded in about 1500 B.C. and qualify as some of the oldest literary endeavours known. Mankind was down from the trees and out of the caves but there remains in these verses a strong sense of the primeval dawn. Their concern is with propitiating the gods of thunder and sun through a system of formalised rites and observations which testify to a tradition ancient even then.

---

* Vedism is the Hinduism of the Vedas, Brahmanism that centred on the godhead Brahman and the supremacy of the Brahmin caste. Saivism is the worship of Siva, Vaishnavism that of Vishnu.

The Aryans proceeded to settle in northern India and to spread first east and then south. Their literary tradition took root and burst into flower with the Upanishads, recorded 800–400 B.C. though composed much earlier, and the epics, the Mahabharata and the Ramayana. The Upanishads taught that the sacrifices of the Vedas were not enough. Man must seek to realise through his own soul the eternal principle of Brahman, the One, the All, the Godhead. The Mahabharata and the Ramayana are more like the Homeric works. The former describes a great battle of gods and men at Kurukshetra in the Punjab. As history it is probably about as factual or fanciful as the Arthurian legends though a good two thousand years earlier. In its most celebrated section, the Bhagavad Gita, the teachings of the Upanishads are taken a step further to allow of a personal love of God. Reminiscent of the Sermon on the Mount and the opening bits of St. John's Gospel this beautiful work has the unsuspecting Christian falling to his knees rather than rising up in arms.

These three collections of works, the Vedas, the Upanishads and the Epics, are the cornerstones of Hinduism, the new and old testaments, and like them they each indicate a rather different personification of the godhead; from Indra and Surya, the nature gods of the Vedas, to Brahman, the metaphysical godhead of the Upanishads, and then Krishna and Rama of the Epics. (The modern trinity of Hinduism represents further development. *Brahma* is the personification of Brahman, *Vishnu* the eternal form of both Rama and Krishna whilst *Siva* is a promoted and renamed version of the Vedic god, Rudra.) From these works, from anthologies and commentaries on them, Hindu belief has evolved. The Upanishads are about as long as the whole Bible and the Mahabharata many times longer making it the world's longest poem. Most people know them only in abbreviated synopses and glosses. And whereas the stories of the Epics, some of the Vedic prayers and a few of the Upanishads are known, along with the Gita, to every educated Hindu, much of these works is the province purely of scholars and theologians.

Having said all this we are still a long way from modern Hinduism and the crowded *ghats* at Benares. The trouble is that the externals of Indian religion are not easily related to the teachings. There is no Koran standardising worship and bridging the gap. How, where and when you practise your religion is almost entirely a question of more recent tradition enshrined in caste *dharma*. And yet it is precisely this practice, these externals, which matter most to Indians. So much so in fact that caste, which sanctioned by the concept of *dharma* becomes a religious institution, controls the whole social life of the country. 'Hinduism,' wrote Dr. Radhakrishna, one of independent India's first presidents, 'is a way of life giving absolute liberty in the world of thought.'

On April 14th 1972 the *Times of India* noted without comment:

> Mr. V. V. Dravid, Vice President of INTUC [the Indian Trades Union Congress] who has been missing for the past nine days, is staying at Rishikesh, engaged in *puja*\* and other religious activities. ... Mr. Dravid has declined to return to public life and expressed his firm determination to devote the rest of his life to religious and spiritual pursuits in Rishikesh.

It was a small piece filling up the bottom of a column. In India renunciations like this are common. Even the toughest politicians and the suavest businessmen are still actively grappling with the basic problems of the meaning of life and the existence of the hereafter. Religion is everywhere. Every big company, every political party has its astrologer. Every shopkeeper turns his premises into a shrine for Divali and with invoice pads, ledgers and ink wells arranged on her altar invokes goddess Lakshmi's intervention to increase the next year's takings. In Bombay the black marketeer marches into his office and while the anxious hippies wait with their few remaining dollars performs a long *puja* to a gyrating image of Siva. And in the Himalayas as rocks hurtle down the hillside on to the road ahead our bus driver skids to a halt, hastily lights a whole bunch of joss sticks, jams them into a holder in front of a large picture of goddess Durga

\* Any Hindu act of worship.

and grimly throws the bus into gear for a wild dash across the landslide.

With so much religion in professional life it is hardly surprising to find even more in family and social life. From the time of the Vedas every Hindu has been born into a caste. Originally there were just four—*Brahmins* (to be distinguished from Brahma, the god, and Brahman, the impersonal godhead), the hereditary priests and interpreters of the Vedas, *Kshatriyas* or later Rajputs, the warriors and princes, *Vaisyas*, the merchants and farmers and *Sudras*, the labourers. The word for caste was *varna* which means 'colour'. The Aryans were fairer than the indigenous population and the caste system was a sort of graded apartheid ensuring the racial purity of the invaders. Every Hindu must marry within his caste and to this day Brahmins in the north can claim to be fairer than most whilst Untouchables and lower castes, sweepers, washermen, etc., are generally darker. The cosmetics industry revolves around the manufacture of creams and potions to lighten the skin pigment and those oft-quoted advertisements for brides and grooms in the *Hindustan Times* invariably insist that the bride is, or must be, of fair complexion.

Since the time of the Vedas the caste system has changed a good deal. The four *varnas* are still recognised but in practice it is the *jati* or sub-caste that matters. As the Aryans spread their influence and numbers throughout the subcontinent the system was widened and diversified to include both subsequent invaders (Huns, Scythians, etc.) and the profusion of indigenous peoples and tribes. This process is still going on; some tribes have a foothold in the lower rungs of caste society while others are still definitely outside it. The original caste functions, Brahmins as priests, Rajputs as warriors, have largely given way to sub-castes with more special-ised occupations though the hierarchy of *varna* still persists. Many Brahmins are cooks or restauranteurs because according to strict caste laws on pollution a Brahmin may only eat food cooked by a Brahmin. Sivaji, the great Hindu warrior, was a Sudra, the Buddha a Kshatriya and so on.

Every *jati* has the most elaborate system of rules which govern every aspect of life. They regulate your status in relation to every other caste, the sort of food you should eat, how and when it should be cooked and how eaten, whom your associates should be, what your profession, who you should marry, how and when, where you should live, the sort of house and how it should be furnished, the clothes you wear, etc., as well as more intimate functions like frequency and method of intercourse, ablutions and excretions. An orthodox Hindu could seemingly live his whole life in accordance with caste *dharma* without taking a single decision. In contemporary practice things are, of course, very different. For one thing caste has nothing to do with wealth. Brahmins of an orthodox bent may be reduced to begging, thus prejudicing their traditional authority at the head of the caste hierarchy. Sudras, even outcastes, may become extremely wealthy thus belying the humility of their caste status. Under the Indian constitution caste is outlawed. This does not mean that it no longer exists; simply that Untouchables are no longer underprivileged in the eyes of the law. Thanks to Mahatma Gandhi the country at least has a social conscience about the deprived. In spite of all this it is usually admitted that caste is really only crumbling in the cities. The demands of urban life mean that taboos must go. Brahmins and Untouchables rub shoulders on the buses, eat in the same office canteen and drink from the same refrigerated water machine. Girls and boys of different caste see the same movies; they learn about that very Western ideal, love, as the basis of marriage and, contrary to the dictates of caste and the censure of family, proceed to get married. So at least the argument goes and for the *élite* westernised upper classes of the major cities it is true. It does not, however, apply to urban life as a whole or to rural life. The caste system is strong enough to adapt and survive for a good bit longer.

On the Bombay metro there are stencilled signs saying 'This carriage reserved for milkmen, vegetable dealers and tiffin carriers'. So even the railways are still discriminating. 'Well not quite,' explains V., as we follow rather cautiously into the carriage.

Only at certain times of the day. And then it's not a question of caste; it's just that they all have rather bulky loads, sacks of radishes and big brass bowls of milk, which might inconvenience the other passengers.

'But are they all separate castes?'

'Of course.'

'Not just anyone can become a milkman in Bombay?'

'He could but where would he get the milk and who would buy it if he wasn't of the right caste?'

'And the tiffin carriers?'

I imagined lots of aproned men with thermos flasks and picnic baskets storming the compartment.

'They too are a caste.'

In fact I was wrong. From Churchgate station at about midday the tiffin carriers emerge. On their heads are long wooden troughs filled with what look like a dozen or so paint tins. I had noticed these troughs, three or four to a barrow, being wheeled through the streets. I assumed the men pushing them were interior decorators on the move. But no, each tin is someone's lunch. The tiffin carrier starts his round in the suburbs collecting tins full of steaming rice and curry from the dutiful wives and duly distributes them an hour later to the desks of flagging husbands. Perhaps after all the multi-caste office canteen is not doing so well. Even in Bombay you can ensure that your food is untouched by low caste hands.

V. himself is a Saraswat Brahmin. He lives in a suburb off Matunga Road and sells industrial concentrates—not a very Brahminical calling. His home is in a block of flats. The several hundred other families who live in his and adjacent blocks are all Saraswats. Downstairs there is a Saraswat Bank Ltd., a Saraswat Launderette and a school run and patronised by Saraswats. Every so often the Saraswat *swami* (religious or caste leader) comes to call. The ladies rush to make sure that their *tilakas* (forehead marks) are of the right size and shade while the Saraswat gents slip out of their city suiting into a *dhoti* (a length of white cotton tied to give the effect of a compromise between skirt and trousers);

The crowds in Chandni Chowk, Old Delhi

A Punjabi Sikh

Swamiji* prefers this traditional apparel. V. has to get the man next door to tie his *dhoti*; he can never make it stay up. And all this in the context of a sub-caste renowned for its adoption of the professions and its general emancipation.

Not only does caste linger on but it continues to proliferate. The leather workers on the road down to the Benares ghats are not all of the same caste. Those who repair shoes consider themselves a stitch or two above those who, dealing in raw leather, actually make shoes. Apparently there is even a caste of chauffeurs and according to one writer the situation is 'almost ripe for a Rolls-Royce caste rejecting food or marriage with a Ford caste'. The proliferation of castes among domestic servants is a continual cause of bemusement to foreigners. The bearer baulks at cleaning anything, the cleaner at cleaning the lavatory and the gardener at sweeping the drive. It seems you cannot run even a modest household without an *ayah, khansama, bearer, chaukidar, chaprassi*,† etc. There has always been something of the Trades Union about the *jati*, the sub-caste. At the Durgapur steel works it was discovered that the furnaces were falling well below their production target because no one was removing the cinders. Waste disposal, like sweeping, has always been a despised occupation and clearly the foundrymen regarded it as below their dignity. Job demarcation is as sure a sign of an emergent new caste as the refusal to marry or take food amongst erstwhile colleagues.

In addition to this evidence of the survival of caste there is a body of opinion‡ which sees the system as beneficial. Against its inequalities must be set the undeniable fact that caste has given to Indian society an unequalled stability enabling it to survive innumerable political upheavals, conquests and economic disasters including six hundred years of Muslim rule, nearly two hundred of British, and currently the attractions of communism. 'As a

---

* The *swami* is a religious or caste leader. The '-ji' suffix signifies respect or affection. Hence Gandhiji, Indiraji, etc.

† *Ayah* is a nanny or ladies' maid, *khansama* a cook, *bearer* a butler or waiter, *chaukidar* a caretaker or watchman and *chaprassi* a messenger. But all these titles vary from one city to another.

‡ See J. H. Hutton, *Caste in India*.

scheme of social adjustment (it) compares rather favourably with the European of warring territorial nationalities' writes W. H. Gilbert. It has accorded to backward and subject peoples a place in society without depriving them of their livelihood and individual way of life—something of a contrast with the American treatment of the Red Indian or the Australian of the Aborigine. And finally it acknowledges the responsibility of the caste for its individual members thus providing the rudimentary benefits of a welfare state. Ideally a caste member may expect from his caste a home if he is an orphan, food if he is unemployed, medical assistance if he is sick, credit in hard times and a free cremation if he dies penniless.

For every infringement of caste law there is a fixed penalty imposed by the caste *panchayat* or council. Two of the commonest such penalties are a pilgrimage to the Ganges, usually at Benares, and the consumption of the *panchgavya*, that is the five products of the cow: milk, curds, *ghi* (clarified butter), dung and urine. The sanctity of the cow and of rivers, especially the Ganges, is as old as Hinduism and, for the visitor, perhaps its most striking features. If you want to understand India look into the face of a Brahminy bull, they all tell you. The humped cattle of India are indeed rather special and in those beautiful eyes below the long lashes one can see a serenity, understanding and patience fully in keeping with the strict observance of *dharma*. The sturdy little black cows of Himachal, the chestnut bulls of Gujerat with their heavy rounded foreheads and the gigantic brahminy cattle of the North—all are holy, protected against slaughter by law, even in some states by the death penalty, and universally acclaimed as the symbols of beneficence and motherhood. This is not always to the cows' benefit. In the Deccan and the South their horns are painted with gold and red and hung with long tickly tassels. The plight of unowned, uncared for and unslaughterable bulls in the big cities is simply to waste away and die of starvation in the middle of the street. Even the truck drivers on the Grand Trunk Road slow for a straying cow and deal patiently with the long streams of bullock carts plodding on, unlighted, their drivers asleep, through the night.

It has been conjectured that this reverence for cattle has in origin something to do with the settling down of the Aryan invaders. Beef which was still being eaten when the Vedas were composed was of less significance to a settled population than the encouragement of dairy produce. Equally it might owe something to the Buddhist abhorrence of any kind of slaughter. However this may be, even today an Indian with a cow is well on the way to self-sufficiency. Milk, *ghi*, curds and buttermilk with various additives are prized as food well above rice, meat or vegetables. Cow dung patted into round cakes by a proud mother and dried in the sun is still the staple fuel in most of the country. It also comes in handy as a substitute for plaster on the walls and floors of most village houses and as a scouring pad for dirty saucepans. Whole books have been written about the efficacy of cow's urine. In remedies for every kind of physical and mental disorder it figures. Beside the products of the cow must be set the usefulness of the bull which is only slightly less holy. (Rather less of this bovine sanctity rubs off on the poor buffalo.) The bull or ox pulls the plough, pulls the ox-cart and often draws the water. In the millions of villages without electricity, cars or tractors this is the only source of power.

The official committee on cow protection, according to the *Times of India* (April 15th 1972) is headed by the retired Chief Justice of India and includes four of the most powerful Chief Ministers (of States), the Animal Husbandry Commissioner, a director of something called the Central Food Technological Research Bureau and, of course, several distinguished *swamis* (religious leaders). One of the watchdogs of Indian society, its aim is not to develop breeding stock and milk yields or to care for unwanted cattle but simply to see that cows are not killed. In 1970 when the Congress Party split, the fiercest controversy raged not over a conflict of ideals and objectives but over the adoption of a party symbol. In politics as in religion the externals are what matter. Mrs. Gandhi's section of the party adopted the cow and calf as their symbol—in a predominantly illiterate society it is the symbol, the lamp, the bicycle, the horseman or the cow, on the ballot paper that most people vote for, not the candidate. The other section of Congress objected saying that the cow was widely recognised as a religious symbol and therefore unacceptable. The matter went to court but by permitting the opposition to adopt the spinning wheel—another strongly evocative symbol given a quasi-religious significance by Mahatma Gandhi—Mrs. Gandhi stole most of the wind from her opponents' sails. When her helicopter descends on his fields for a quick bit of electioneering the peasant is often reported as having proclaimed her as the goddess Durga come down to save the cow and the calf.

If the cattle of India are somehow special so too are the rivers. There is no need to harp on the significance of water in a country like India but what makes the rivers, particularly in the North, so different is that like the goddess Kali (another form of Durga who is another form of Parvati, wife of Siva) they have a terrifying as well as a beneficial aspect. The Ganges, the Jumna, the Brahmaputra and their tributaries are all rivers in search of a bed. When the monsoon is heavy and the snows of the Himalayas melting, floods are inevitable. The usually peaceful rivers start to swell and froth, to flood and change course. Well-irrigated fields are left high and dry miles from the river that watered them, others are inundated. Whole villages are made or ruined. Flying from Delhi to Benares or Calcutta you can see the vast swathe of the Ganges. It's like a tangled skein of rivers strewn at random across the plain. No towns cluster along its banks, no towpaths or embankments, just gentle sand dunes affording the freedom to roam wherever it pleases. Delhi is on the Jumna but you could live there for years without seeing the river or knowing of its existence. It has slunk quietly away from the ramparts of the Red Fort into a no-man's land of vegetation and rubble. At Allahabad there is a festival every twelve years called the Kumbh Mela. It takes place at the confluence of the three rivers, the Jumna, the Ganges and the Saraswati. But there are only two; the Saraswati has disappeared.

# The North (2)

Benares is one of the few places where the Ganges has settled for a regular course. Deserting its predominantly south-easterly flow it swings due north and up past the holy city. On the right-hand bank there are the usual sand dunes and flat waste land but on the left rise the famous bathing steps (ghats) with above them a chaotic skyline of cupola-ed palaces, temple *sikharas*,* even minarets and Buddhist pagodas with the occasional glimpse of a golden spire. The sun rises out of the flat waste land in the east. First, like the solitary spotlight of some grand 'son-et-lumière', it strikes the minaret and golden spire, then the palaces and temples and slowly down the steep ghats to the water's edge. This is the moment for spiritual renewal. Brown bodies, old and young, fat and thin, plunge into the sparkling waters. The air is filled with the hum of prayer and away towards Dufferin Bridge goes a flotilla of jasmine and marigold flowers, the offerings of the faithful.

Up and down in front of the ghats glides an assortment of craft, rowing boats and big two-tiered motor launches packed with sightseers. Like cruising sharks they pause to feint with whirring cines and clicking Nikons before a plump Bengali lady in trouble with her billowing sari or a waist-deep ascetic standing motionless with a cup of Ganges water raised to the sun. For us, chastened by many months of experience into a deep respect for India and its religion, it was too much like sacrilege. Our boatman pulled obligingly upstream for a closer look at the less commercialised spectacles.

Here in Benares the threads of Hinduism and of India, like the tangled skein of the Ganges itself, begin to fall into place. The Brahmin, his sacred thread slung diagonally across the body from shoulder to hip and his *tikki*, a hank of long hair, now wet and hanging from crown to nape, is chanting the *gayatri*, most famous of the Vedic verses. Near by a saddhu with long matted hair, his body smeared with ash and his eyes glazed by drugs, sits cross-legged and motionless. Across his knees is a trident to distinguish

* Spires but seldom very high or pointed.

55

him as a follower of Lord Siva, Siva from whose hair the sacred river flows high on Mount Kailas in the Himalayas and to whom the city of Benares is dedicated. But sectarianism stops there. In the holy city everyone has a place. There is a bathing ghat for Muslims, another patronised by Jains, and still more for pilgrims from the South, for Bengalis and for Rajputs. The gilding on the Golden Temple was courtesy of Ranjit Singh, the great emperor of the Punjab. The mosque whose minarets pierce the otherwise Hindu skyline is a legacy of the bigoted Aurangzeb. It stands on the site of a temple he destroyed to make way for it. The later ghats are the gifts of the great Mahratta houses—that of Scindia boasts a wind shelter like those on Eastbourne esplanade. Even if the sahibs never built themselves a ghat there is to the north that far more representative monument, the Dufferin Bridge. Aloof and unconcerned it bears across the sacred river the symbols of the White Man's bounty, the railway and the Grand Trunk Road.

Above the ghats is a maze of narrow streets crowded with cattle and pilgrims. Dodging the piles of precious cow dung a party of Gujerati peasants in heavy clumping shoes and bulky turbans come clattering over the cobbles. They are late for the sunrise; back home in Saurashtra it rises a good hour later than here. We wandered on into the maze still pursued by the boatman anxious to elicit another rupee. Changing tactics he ushered us into a doorway behind which the celebrated silk saris of Benares, all gold and red, were being woven on handlooms. The rupee forgotten we plunged on for the Golden Temple. One expected the street to debouch suddenly on to a piazza with 'il duomo' captive in the midst. But no. 'This Golden Temple.' One could walk straight past without realising. From inside came the sounds and smells of *puja*. A bell is rung to alert Visvesvara (Siva) of the pilgrim's arrival. A handful of sweet-smelling blooms are scattered over the bull Nandi, Siva's mount. The *pujari* (priest) intones a prayer and waves a bowl of blazing camphor oil before the lingam, Siva's phallic symbol. Small bells tinkle, a coco-nut and a few bananas are offered to the god and then distributed.

Animated and anointed with bright daubs of *kunkum* powder the
pilgrims reassemble and head off for the next shrine. It is all very
gay and noisy. Piety and sanctity in the solemn Christian sense
have no place here.

I still had the same feeling when later we faced, across a few
feet of water, the burning ghats. Two or three funeral pyres
were blazing brightly in the morning sun. Another body carried
precariously down the steps on a stretcher and covered with pink
cloth—'Pink means woman' said the boatman—was waiting its
turn. The body burners I expected to be like those ghouls in
illustrations of the Inferno but they looked sober and busy. They
were neither noticeably exultant like the prancing ghouls nor
oppressively sanctimonious like an undertaker. Not a bad way to
go, I reflected. Quicker than the worms of the grave or the vultures of the Towers of Silence and far more cheerful. Another
pyre went up with a dry whoosh of flame, the water lapped at
the lower logs and the sun went on shining—an elemental scene.
If there is a short cut to Nirvana, Benares seemed a good stepping-
off point.

One is tempted to ask how much in all this the Hindu sincerely
believes. Do the pilgrims believe that their visit to Benares wipes
out all previous transgressions, do the mourners honestly believe
that the figure on the pyre is achieving eternal deliverance? Is
there any eternal deliverance? Are the exploits of Krishna and
Rama really true and is the cow really holy? The gullibility of
Indians is considerable but to ascribe to this the Indian acceptance
of so much myth and taboo is to miss the point. The power of the
supernatural and the meaning of life are things to be felt rather
than rationalised. The beauty rather than the logic of any belief
or taboo is what counts. And the spirit of worship is in its dutiful
performance rather than the supplicant's sincerity. Siva's phallic
symbol is a symbol not a phallus. Most Hindus would be deeply
shocked if you suggested they were worshipping a sex organ.
So, too, would the village clergyman if you accused him of
idolising beans and marrows at the harvest festival. Both are just
symbols of fertility and bounty. So, too, the cows and the rivers.

## . . . *And an Ancient Patrimony*

They mean more in India because India is still an overwhelmingly agricultural country. The yield of livestock and field means not just higher or lower incomes but the difference between subsistence and starvation in the perilous lives of the poor. No wonder they take their symbols seriously.

# 4. A MADHOUSE OF RELIGIONS

## The South

Outside a Bombay art gallery the posters announced a photographic exhibition of the architectural monuments of southern India. The headline read 'January 25th 1565—The Day The Real India Died'. They referred to Vijayanagar, the last great Hindu empire of the South, which on that date was routed following the battle of Talikota, a veritable Hastings in the history of peninsular India. The period is that of the final stage of Muslim conquest in India. In the North Akbar was beginning his long reign of conquest but in the South it was his semi-independent satellites, the Muslim kingdoms of Bijapur, Berar and Golconda who faced across the Krishna and Tunghabhadra rivers the for-once-united forces of the Hindu South. At stake was thousands of years of Hindu rule in the South and an independent way of life which had orientated the southern states more towards the outside world of Ceylon, South-East Asia and the Arabian Sea than Delhi or the North. In the ensuing rout the Hinduism of the South survived but its political peninsularity was at an end. From 1565 onwards the area was drawn progressively into the main stream of Indian history. The Moghuls, Shah Jehan and Aurangzeb, asserted their sovereignty over the Muslim invaders and extended their rule well beyond Madras. The Mahrattas followed suit and the British with their genius for communications and a standardised administration finally erased the political definition of the South.

But as a geographical, racial and cultural entity the empire of Vijayanagar and the concept of southern India which it represented still remain. From the Krishna river south, things start to look different. For a start there are two monsoons. Heavy rains in both summer and early winter give the coastal areas a luxuriant greenness which never fades. The rivers are more reliable and even the dry plateau country of Mysore is well served with lakes, reservoirs and ponds. The monotony of green and brown is everywhere shattered by splashes of reflected blue sky. White and red lilies, carpets of blue water hyacinth and tall lotus draw the brilliant turquoise kingfishers and elegant white egrets. The scenery changes with very un-Indian rapidity. Along the east coast the sand dunes are dotted with lonely palmyra palms whilst in the west the breakers of the Arabian Sea crash over fine beaches straight into the shaggy coco-nut groves. In between there are forests of teak, their gigantic leaves waving like lazy elephant's ears, mountains alight with the blazing 'flame of the forest' trees, rocky slopes of hopeless desolation and jungle clearings where small villages nestled amid their patchwork fields, live out their isolated existence.

The people too are different. For one thing they are not Aryans but Dravidians, a people who inhabited the subcontinent long before the Aryans invaded the North and whose languages to this day are totally different. Here as elsewhere in India the formation of the present-day states has been based on these linguistic distinctions so that the four southern states, Mysore, Andhra Pradesh, Tamil Nadu (Madras) and Kerala correspond to the four Dravidian languages of respectively Kannada, Telugu, Tamil and Malayalam. If one thinks of India as being the same size as Europe less Russia it is not surprising to find such variations. The script, grammar and vocabulary of say Tamil are as foreign to a Bihari as Greek is to a Scandinavian. Place names and surnames run to dozens of syllables. Mr. Venkataramana Muthukrishna Mathru-bhuteswaran of Sankaranayinerkovil in Tirunelveli District does you great honour by introducing himself; it is not something he undertakes lightly. The Dravidian peoples are the Latins of India. They are shorter, more volatile and benefit from a richer cultural tradition. Instead of a *dhoti* tied through the legs the men wear a *lungi*, a length of material usually coloured tied round the waist like a towel and often hitched up like a sarong. Their hair is more

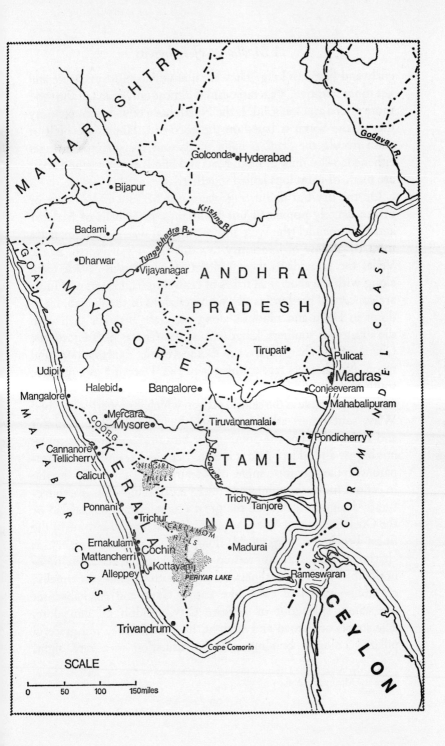

curly and faces less long. They are if anything more excitable and yet more sensitive. Vegetarianism is almost universal and the food more spiced and less solid. If the North has a cow-based economy that of the South is based on the coco-nut. Houses are built of palm fronds, the drink is palm toddy and every recipe includes either coco-nut milk or flesh. Mats and blinds are of coir and boats are made of palm logs lashed together.

On the dry but undulating plateau of Mysore and Andhra or in the densely populated but luxuriant coastal belts of Malabar and Coromandel (the west and east coasts) one is struck perhaps most by a sense of inferiority towards the Aryan North. In the Vedas the Dravidians were written off as 'Dasyus', black men, along with the aboriginal tribes of central India. Histories of India are concerned predominantly with invasions of the Punjab, kingdoms in Delhi and mutinies along the Ganges rather than with the illustrious southern kingdoms of the Cholas of Tanjore, the Cheras of Malabar, Pallavas of Conjeeveram (Kanchipuram) and so on. Northerners talk scathingly of the 'Deccan'\* as anywhere south of Agra and imply that the whole of the peninsula is as arid and unproductive as the central plateau which it properly describes. Why, southerners ask, are tourists always directed to Kashmir and Benares? Is not the South more beautiful and are its temples not bigger and older? And it is true. Benares has nothing to compare with the gigantic temples of Madurai and Tanjore. Khajuraho in central India, though famed for its erotic sculptures, is architecturally insignificant beside the great Hoysaleswara of Halebid or the Great Temple of Vijayanagar. In Kerala one finds some of the finest beaches in the world along with mountain scenery as charming if not as impressive as the Himalayas. Even more noticeable is the cleanliness of the South. Beside the smelly, crumbling chaos of cities like Patna, Gaya and Allahabad set the stately splendour of Mysore City, Madras or Bangalore. The streets are broad and straight, lined with trees and graceful pillared colonial buildings. Public urination is a rare sight.

---

\* Strictly speaking the Deccan is the higher inland areas of Mysore, Andhra, Maharashtra and Madhya Pradesh.

The talk over coffee and a Trichy cheroot at Spencers on that unequalled thoroughfare, Mount Street in Madras, is of plantations in the Cardamom Hills or the latest Malayalam movie.

In 1966 the flames of North–South antipathy flared up over the language issue. The Census records that Indians speak a staggering 1549 different languages.* Of these some fourteen are officially recognised for administrative purposes but since independence India has been in search of one common language for central affairs and public examinations. English would be the simplest solution were the country able to swallow its pride and officially endorse a foreign language. But Hindi, the language of the North which is understood by about a quarter of the population and is at least recognisable to a fair number of others, Punjabis and Bengalis included, was to be adopted as the nearest thing to a national tongue. This provoked an uproar in the South. For at least a century English and Tamil had been accepted as good enough for all official purposes. Here English is more widely spoken than elsewhere in India and for the Dravidian it is as easy to master as Hindi. Tamil has close links with the other southern languages and boasts a literary heritage far richer than Hindi. Militant Dravidian parties, notably the Tamil D.M.K. party, rocketed to prominence in defence of the vernacular and of all things southern. In the elections in Tamil Nadu they routed the Congress Party which, then sadly in need of allies, dropped the Hindi issue in return for the D.M.K.'s support. In Madras the hero of the moment was Annadurai, founder of the D.M.K. His portrait, which is easily mistaken for Sheikh Mujibur Rahman, still hangs in most tea shops and offices, a face of great character and, I was assured, great integrity. His *samadhi*† on Marine Drive is as well attended as that of Mahatma Gandhi in Delhi. Sadly the D.M.K. is not now the party it was. It still raises the cry of greater autonomy for the states, or at least for Tamil Nadu, but Annadurai

* The 1961 Census of India. Most of these are unwritten tribal tongues.

† A difficult word. Properly speaking it refers to a state of union with the godhead. Yogis strive to realise it through physical disciplines but most hope to achieve it only in death. Hence it also comes to mean the place of death or, as in this case, of cremation.

is gone and typically Indian corruption has set in. Why are there fishermen camped along the beach of Madras's Marine Drive? Because access to this piece of coast was the price the D.M.K. paid for their vote in the last election. And why, the press were asking, were obscene floor shows being permitted to sully the decorous night life of Madras? Was this a new D.M.K. scheme for fund raising?

With the language issue currently shelved there are plenty of other bones of contention. In scholarly circles 1972 saw a row brewing over the earliest of India's civilisations, that of the Indus Valley found at Harappa and Mohenjo-daro and excavated by Sir Mortimer Wheeler. It had been a considerable boost to Dravidian sensibilities when by general agreement the civilisation was chalked up to the early Dravidian peoples. It indicated not only that they once, some three thousand years ago, enjoyed a standard of civilisation rather higher than that of the Aryans but also that they too contributed to the corpus of tradition and taboo which is Hinduism today. Sanskrit literature would have us believe that Hinduism was an Aryan creation which had to be foisted on the reluctant spirit worshippers of the subcontinent. In fact vital elements like worship of the lingam were Harappan and therefore Dravidian contributions. The Aryan peoples of the North and more especially their Sanskrit scholars have never been happy about this award and decided, with that great Indian disregard for fact, to 'initiate research into the Indus Valley civilisation as a reflection of Aryan culture'. Not only is it generally accepted that Harappa and other cities flourished well before the Aryans arrived, but that if there is a connection it is that the Aryans were the destroyers of this civilisation. The Madras edition of the *Indian Express* put it mildly when in an editorial it said 'Historical research of this type cannot be sound scholarship'. I wondered whether the same editorial appeared in Delhi editions of the paper.

With this upsurge of local sentiment scholars have gone foraging into records and ruins to resurrect the almost forgotten glories of Hindu rule in the South before the peninsula was submerged in the subcontinent. Kerala, formed in 1956 out of the western seaboard of the Madras Presidency* and the princely states of Malabar, was named after the ancient Chera kings of that district. In Tamil Nadu you can travel by road on a Pandyan Roadways or a Pallavan Roadways bus—or indeed take the Pandyan Express. It is all a bit artificial though there is no doubting the one-time significance of these ancient Dravidian kingdoms. Solomon and Ptolemy looked to the Malabar coast for peacocks, pearls and peppercorns just as did Greeks and Romans. Caesar Augustus received ambassadors from the Pandyas in Madurai who, like the Cheras, employed Roman soldiers as a bodyguard. Much later the Chola kings conquered Ceylon and colonised in Burma, Cambodia and the East Indies. The Angkhor Wat and the Hindu temples of Bali stem from this period of Tamil expansion. Finally we have the ruins and the temples, Tanjore, Madurai, Conjeeveram and, later, Halebid and Vijayanagar. These are not the creations of fly-by-night princelings. The abundance of good building stone and the flagging iconoclasm of the Muslims has left the South far better endowed with ancient buildings than any part of India. At Tiruvannamalai in Tamil Nadu there is a gigantic temple, bigger than, though contemporary with, Madurai. It stands complete and still very much in use but no guide book accords it so much as a mention. In the South there are just too many such places.

It is a curious feature of contemporary India that just as greater unity and centralisation have occasioned an upsurge of regional and caste sentiments so the adoption of progressive and Western ideals—democracy, economic planning, etc.—have been matched by a determined revivalism. Mahatma Gandhi dug into tradition for his ideals of *ahimsa* (non-violence) and *varnashradharma* (the original caste system) as well as advocating a return to the self-sufficient and self-governing village community with its own *panchayat* or council. There has been a revival of Sanskrit studies and an unprecedented spate of historical and archaeological

* The Madras Presidency was one of the three Presidencies into which British India was divided. Bengal and Bombay were the other two.

research. The great temple of Madurai has been painted in garish reds, greens and yellows. Sacrilege, I thought, but then someone assured me that that was how it was originally intended to be. Democracy, one is told, is a traditional Indian ideal. What were the *panchayats* if not democratic? Even the aeroplane and the H-bomb are not Western inventions. Apparently somewhere deep in the Sanskrit classics references may be found to suggest that the ancient Aryans knew of both.

To my mind better by far than the restored prettiness of Madurai is the wild neglect of Vijayanagar. Somehow the greatness of the past is more impressive in abandon. At first glance it is difficult to tell where the ruins start and the surrounding boulder-strewn scarps end. The impression of appalling chaos and desolation is heightened by lush fields of sugar cane, products of the Tunghabhadra irrigation scheme, which choke the low-lying perimeter of the site. In its day the great city was twenty-four miles round. It contained palaces of marble, colossal stone elephant stables, delicate ladies' pavilions, baths, bazaars, ceremonial gateways and, of course, hundreds of temples. The destruction of such a place where scarcely a stone can be lifted without crowbars and tackle was a feat comparable with its erection. Now, more even than Akbar's deserted city of Fatehpur Sikri,* Vijayanagar has atmosphere. Few people go there and those that do must stay some miles away at a rest house run by the Tunghabhadra Hydro Project. Mostly the ruins are deserted. A few skinny Deccan cattle graze amongst the fallen aqueducts. The Ancient Monuments Board have been busy with their signs about not defacing the stones, but villages for miles around seem to be built from the big granite paving slabs of the city. A wind busies itself on the crumbling hillsides and big horny lizards scuttle into crevices on the King's Throne. In what Murray's *Handbook to India* calls 'The King's or Ladies' Bath' (together?) frogs are sporting in the shallows. Perhaps not the Real India but something, an

---

* A few miles from Agra. Fatehpur Sikri was deserted, probably due to a shortage of water, shortly after its construction. It was never sacked and is therefore in a fine state of preservation.

The bathing ghats at Benares

The pool and gopurams of the Great Temple at Madurai

extravagant unshakeable outlook founded on tradition rather than conviction, took a tumble at Talikota. The South has never quite recovered from it.

*      *      *

The 'Real India' even if it survives is something of an illusion. Every Peace Corps worker after a few months in Rajasthan, Bihar or Mysore thinks he knows it, but the real India is no more there than the real Europe is in France, Poland or Norway. The South never was the real India but it is, even today, a must for anyone seeking to understand the Indian character. In its hot-house atmosphere peculiarly Indian features and institutions become more pronounced and exaggerated. Tenacious little communities, anachronistic castes and semi-tribal clans proliferate in a climate of religious fervour and social rigidity matched only by the vegetational riot of the coastal belts and the timeless beauty of the rolling Deccan plateau. Nowhere is this more so than in Kerala, the most densely populated, highly educated and politically unpredictable of the Indian states. Inland the mountains are swathed in rich rubber, coffee and tea plantations, with pepper, cardamom and areca (betel) nut, but on the coastal belt the palm trees take over. Here amidst the endless maze of swaying trunks and tossing, feathered fronds scored by countless canals lives one of the world's most oddly assorted populations. It's like a cross between the Levantine and Californian coasts. Christians, Jews, Muslims and Hindus all of the most orthodox persuasion live cheek by jowl in a unique harmony.

A stroll through the bazaars of Cochin gives some idea of the cosmopolitan atmosphere. Kenneth Galbraith, Kennedy's ambassador in India, compared its situation to that of San Francisco with Ernakulam as Oakland and the harbour as the Bay. Through the harbour mouth—no Golden Gate Bridge here—dhows, blistered tramp steamers, three- and four-masted sailing ships and big modern cargo vessels heave in and out on the tides. Inside the harbour ferries and ramshackle 'country' boats are dashing about between Cochin, Ernakulam and the many islands. Turning from the harbour mouth we faced the church of St. Francis with around it the quiet fort area of tiled, slightly concave Dutch roofs. The Church of St. Francis is dedicated to the Catholic missionary St. Francis Xavier; but it is Protestant. Outside there is a British war memorial, inside most of the inscriptions are in Dutch and somewhere there is supposed to be the tomb of Vasco da Gama. It's all very puzzling. A big hairy man in a short-sleeved white shirt approaches. He is not Indian; perhaps he is Portuguese and also looking for da Gama. No. 'Georgian.' It sounded improbable but yes, he was from the Republic of Georgia. Off a ship? No, he was a musician from Calcutta. The plot thickened. He was in Cochin on business, came often from Calcutta and he was sorry his English was not better. Usually he spoke Georgian. Of course.

'Cochin is beautiful,' I ventured.

No, he replied, he lived in Calcutta, but Georgia between the Black Sea and Caucasus was his home. He had to go now. Vasco da Gama had been taken back to Portugal but his tomb is over there.

'Thank you and good-bye'.

'No mention it, good-bye'.

The chaotic cosmopolitanism of Cochin was clearly not just of the past. We found the tomb and managed to work out the history of the Church. Portuguese, then Dutch, then British was the succession of colonial powers in Cochin and of worshippers at St. Francis. The Portuguese left da Gama's tomb but the Church itself was destroyed and rebuilt by the Dutch. The British added just the war memorial and a set of fine *punkahs* (fans) some thirty feet long which can safely be pulled by a heathen because the pull ropes pass clean through the outside walls to a shadeless spot among the buttresses.

On next to the Cathedral of Santa Cruz to which we were directed by a Muslim tailor on his round of the big houses. If he was a local Muslim then probably he was a Moplah. Arab traders had been visiting the Malabar coast long before Mohammed, in the seventh century, put the fear of Allah into them. They controlled the trade routes of the Arabian Sea, knew all about the monsoon winds, and had installed small Arab communities from Gujerat to Cape Comorin. The Moplahs of Kerala, their descendants, were probably the first Muslims in India and they remain a distinct and fanatical sect. Chiefly resident in Calicut, Ponani and Cannanore they spread round the peninsula and small communities are also found on the Coromandel coast. Those at Pulicat, another Dutch colony, read the Koran in Tamil, a curious irregularity amongst a community usually distinguished for its orthodoxy. It would be wrong to say that these far-flung adherents of Islam had always lived in peace with their fellow Hindus and Christians; even in 1972 riots between Hindus and Muslims were in progress just up the coast at Tellicherry. Across the bay in Ernakulam the mobile vasectomy unit was in town. Sixty-five thousand men stepped forward of whom only one hundred and twenty were Muslim. The mullahs had forbidden sterilisation. But in Kerala as a whole, where the Muslim population is close on thirty per cent, there was no serious rioting during the partition crisis in 1947 as there was in Bengal and Punjab. Kerala's Muslims are still far closer to the Arab world than to the Mohammedanism of Pakistan.

The Cathedral of Santa Cruz was positively Roman Catholic but even Rome, in the mixed-up world of the Malabar coast, is not just one religion. There are two rites, Syrian and Latin, not to mention the non-Roman churches. The confusion all started because southern India is one of the few places outside Palestine where Christianity arrived before it became identified with Rome. It began with a mysterious Thomas who founded what is called the Syrian Church of South India. Whether he was really the doubting Thomas of the twelve apostles it is impossible to say but he certainly existed and brought Christianity to India.* His tomb is at San Thome in Madras and the church he founded is well

---

* The Cambridge History of India quotes, from the Apocryphal Acts of the Apostles II, a delightful piece about Thomas' reluctance to go to India. 'Whithersoever thou wilt Lord, send me; but to India I will not go.' Eventually he had to be sold to a visiting Indian who was looking for a carpenter to take home with him.

attested in places of worship predating the arrival of European Christianity by some centuries. A church or school dedicated to St. Francis Xavier is always Roman Catholic but one dedicated to St. Thomas is immediately identifiable as Syrian Orthodox. Around Cochin, Ernakulam, Alleppey and Trivandrum the Syrian Christians represent a quarter of the population. The telephone directory is full of surnames like George, John, Peter and Joseph and in the bazaars Christian women, more emancipated and educated than their Hindu sisters, are much in evidence. Dressed in a rather Chinese outfit of tight white blouse and white *lungi* with hair swept tightly back to show off their enormous gold ear-rings they fill Cochin with the rather un-Indian frivolity of a Parisian market.

Like the Muslims of the North or the caste-conscious Hindus, the Christians of Kerala are riddled with schism. Until Vasco da Gama and the Portuguese made their first settlement in India in 1502 they were simply the Syrian Christians of South India. Syrian, because like most other Eastern Christians they recognised the authority of the Nestorian Patriarchs of Babylon rather than the Bishop of Rome. Mastering their pique at finding these far-flung believers, the Portuguese set about ridding them of their Nestorianism and more especially of their devotion to Babylon rather than to Rome. Those who rejected this approach are now members of what is called the Chaldean Church of India; they are to be found chiefly round Trichur and still look to their Babylonian, i.e. Syrian, patriarch who now lives in the U.S.A., But many succumbed to the Portuguese pressure and constitute the present community of the Syrian rite of the Roman Catholic Church in India. How simple it would be if it ended there. Christians they were and still are but this was a Church of Indians rather than foreigners; inevitably fragmentation continued. Angered by the Portuguese waylaying a Persian Bishop who was hastening to the scene on behalf of Babylon a large number of those who had gone over to Rome changed their minds. They took a solemn oath on the Crooked Cross,* a common sight

---

* The Syrian cross is not so much crooked as askew and usually represented on its side.

round Alleppey, and formed the Syrian Orthodox Church of India. In 1665 a Bishop did at last get through the Portuguese blockade but unfortunately he represented not Babylon but another Eastern patriarchate, Antioch. We called at one of his churches founded in 722 according to the bearded orthodox priest but now under the authority of the 'Patrick of Andokia'. Known as the Jacobite Church the Antioch patriarchs embraced the Monophysite heresy rather than that of Nestorius. Such theological niceties were lost on the Indians—one suspects they had had enough for the time being—and so things remained until the nineteenth century when some of the Crooked Cross followers severed contact with Antioch and set up their own Catholicos or supreme bishop. Further schisms have arisen since and, as with the Muslims, even within some communities a caste system militates for still greater confusion. An example is provided by the fishermen of Malabar. Appropriately they proved willing converts but were reluctant to shed their caste and trade distinctions completely. So today those who cast their nets from boats will be predominantly Syrian rite Roman Catholics, those who operate the big Chinese scoop nets Syrian Orthodox and those who fish from the beach Latin rite Roman Catholics.

Beside the Catholic and Syrian churches, Kerala has more than its fair share of Protestant churches. Missionaries, Lutheran, Baptist, Methodist, Anglican, Seventh-Day Adventist and Jehovah's Witness recognising Kerala as one of the world's greatest free ports where doctrine was concerned are all well represented. There are whole streets of nothing but churches and half the population seems to be in holy orders. Bishops, Archbishops, Cardinals and Catholicos' are two a penny. If you have a new religion to impart to the world nowhere will you find a more promising seedbed than in Kerala. The roads are lined with shrines and even the trucks, decorated in the best Indian fashion, sport bold dedications above the cab not just to 'Lord Krishna' or 'Shree Lakshmi' but to 'Hail Mary', 'Lord Jesus', 'God is Love' and 'We Three Kings'. Nuns are so plentiful that they are now being exported to Italy, a recurrent scandal in the Indian press, and yet nurses and teachers in Kerala still find work hard to come by unless they embrace the habit. The Kerala Congress Party—as opposed to the National Congress of Mrs. Gandhi—is predominantly Christian and though, like the Muslims, all Christian groups rarely unite, it occasionally enjoys office in one of the state's ever changing coalition governments.

Already exhausted though we had covered only churches we hailed a cycle rickshaw for the trip to Mattancheri, the native quarter of Cochin. Our cyclist looked like Emperor Haile Selassie. I was prepared to bet that he was a Copt but decided that we had had our fill of Christian denominations. We plunged into Mattancheri and the air became thick with the spicy smells of a Malabar port. I recognised pepper and nutmeg but as for cardamom, ginger, cloves and areca I couldn't be sure. Suddenly we were in a Brahmin quarter surrounded by shaven heads and sacred threads slung across fleshy, hairless chests. They sat cross-legged in front of bales of cloth, drinking tea and chewing betel nut, their lips livid with its red juice. Surely these were not the strictly orthodox Nambudiri Brahmins of Kerala? No, replied our sweating Emperor, they were renegade Tamil Brahmins; Nambudiris would not engage in trade. Even this news was slightly shocking. The Brahmins of the South are supposed to be the most orthodox in India. There are four main groups, the Madhwas of Mysore, the Ayyars and Ayengars of Tamil Nadu and the Nambudiris of Kerala; but each of these, like every other caste, is subdivided into innumerable sects according to which of the Vedas they follow, from whence they originated and with whom they are permitted to intermarry. Strict in the observance of Brahminical rites and of caste aloofness the southern Brahmins rather than be reduced to a totally unworthy status as labourers or beggars have gone in for literature, law, politics and science.

The outspoken firebrand of Keralan politics is E. M. S. Namboodiripad (a surname often indicates a man's caste), leader of Kerala's Marxist Communist Party, the first communist party in the world to be democratically elected to power. Of the Ayyars the novelist R. K. Narayan★ is one of the most distinguished. His short tales of Malgudi, an imaginary township somewhere between Trichy (Tiruchirappali or Trichinopoly) and Mysore City ('the Narayan country') make the traveller's ideal reading matter and give an insight into small town life which years of residence could hardly better. As for the Madhwas of Mysore their headquarters is the town of Udipi near Mangalore. Its *maths* or Brahminical monasteries customarily feed all Madhwa visitors free of charge. On festive days the number of free diners may rise to hundreds of thousands. Udipi Madhwas soon master the skills of mass catering and many have decided to employ them in a more commercial setting. Udipi Brahmin restaurants are found in all the cities of the Deccan and the South from Bombay to Madurai. Inevitably there is one in Mattancheri road. Strictly vegetarian, scrupulously clean and usually very cheap they specialise in South Indian delicacies like *idli* (rice balls) and *dosai* (crisp stuffed pancakes) as well as the more standard rice, curds and coco-nut based vegetable curries.

From the Udipi restaurant by the Dutch Palace—a gift to the Rajas of Cochin—it's only a few yards to the Jewish quarter. Unlike the Christian communities the Jews are few in number and concentrated entirely in Cochin and Ernakulam. They too claim centuries of residence on the Malabar coast and are hopelessly disunited. The Black Jews, the largest community, are descended from Jewish settlers who arrived about the fourth century A.D. and intermarried with the local population. The White Jews coming rather later resisted the local brides and are if anything whiter today than when they first arrived. Even a few red beards may be seen amongst them—perhaps the origin of the 'Brown Jews' of whom no more than their existence is recorded. In the narrow street which leads to the White Jews' synagogue two hopelessly mongol children of a ghostly white were being hustled along by a waxen-faced old lady with a fine semitic nose; the nameplates on the doors announced Dr. Elias, Mr

★ Author of *The English Teacher, The Guide, The Man-Eater of Malgudi* and many other touching and unforgettable characters.

73

Cohen. 'What of the Black Jews', I asked. 'Gone to Israel,' said the old man in the synagogue. Someone else says most of them came back; Israel was too colour conscious for them. Now they are somewhere near the bus stand in Ernakulam. Only Mr. Koder whose chain of stores is represented in every Kerala town seems to be doing well. Otherwise I found these communities rather depressing. Nowhere in the world have Jews been so happily accommodated or so long saved from persecution but somehow they have never prospered. Perhaps the ready acceptance accorded all communities in Kerala is less conducive to hard graft than more hostile settings.

A social climate which for thousands of years allowed such different communities to live in peace is something almost unprecedented. St. Thomas was supposedly martyred but one must look to the Portuguese proponents of the Inquisition before one finds another case of native persecution. Hinduism is not a crusading religion. By being born into a certain caste an Indian is born a Hindu; there is no other way of initiation and the idea of conversion is therefore meaningless. But so basic is caste to religion that the Hindu is happy to recognise another man's birthright to his religion. The Christians, Jews and Moplahs are not of course castes but to the Indian way of thinking they are certainly approximations. And however despised and discriminated against, they are entitled to their religion and bound to their *dharma* just as is the Sudra and the Untouchable or the donkey and the fly.

This extraordinary harmony makes more sense when seen against the background of the Hindu majority in the South. 'A madhouse of caste' was how Vivekananda, the man who first popularised Hinduism in the West, described Kerala but it could just as well apply to the whole of the South. Nowhere else in India does one find so many castes and such minute caste distinctions. Brahmin castes continue to dominate society whilst at the bottom of the scale there are not just Untouchables but Unseeables. Like lepers these Nayadis carry a bell to warn of their approach. On a farm owned by a Syrian Christian family, the Nayadis wages were left in their bowls at the edge of a field whence they were expected to collect them when everyone was well out of sight. For Untouchables the respective distances to within which they may approach a Brahmin, Sudra, etc., are painstakingly recorded and still in rural areas observed. There are Tamil castes who may not carry an umbrella and others who may not live under a tiled roof. Camped near the house where we were staying in Dharwar, Mysore, were a community of extremely poor and scruffy Untouchables.

'A criminal caste,' said G. 'The police moved them here to the edge of the town so that they could keep an eye on them. Robbers mostly.'

Around Vijayanagar we were struck by a community whose women, instead of a local sari the colour of a faded rupee note, were dressed in brilliant patchwork skirts, a loose red and much embroidered bib covering their breasts. Jewellery cascaded from their unbrushed hair, and arms, up to the shoulder, were plated in thick ivory bracelets. Feeling like ardent bird-watchers we looked them up in Thurston.* They were Lambadis, a caste or tribe (the distinction is blurred except when talking of the truly aboriginal peoples) peculiar to the Deccan and who specialised in the carrying trade but are now largely pedlars.

For size and organisation few Indian castes can compare with the Nairs of Kerala. In origin they were Sudras but traditionally found employment as soldiers in the armies of the South. The ancient Chera rulers made of them a sort of Samurai suicide squad and even the Indian Army of the British included a Nair brigade. Through the Nair Service Society their influence on affairs of state is considerable and their internal organisation unequalled. Besides the interminable Mr. Nairs, or Nayars, most of the Menons including Mrs. Nehru's Defence Minister Krishna Menon, are members of this caste. Another distinctive feature of the Nairs is the tradition of inheritance through the women of the family. This phenomenon is found only in some of the Himalayan peoples and here in the South amongst the Nairs and their

* *Castes and Tribes of Southern India.* Edgar Thurston.

neighbours to the north, the Coorgis of Mysore. The Coorgis too have a distinguished military tradition (two of independent India's Chiefs of General Staff have been Coorgis)* but in other respects are an altogether exceptional people, as anomalous as the Jews, the Moplahs or the Nayadis but very much a part of the crazy social composition of the South.

Coorg is the south-western extremity of Mysore, a land of jungle-choked ravines opening as you climb up to Mercara, the capital, on to shady coffee plantations fenced with huge poinsettias, hibiscus and heliotrope which in turn give way to ridge upon ridge of bare hillside receding into the haze. The houses are whitewashed beneath low tiled roofs but large enough to house the clan-like Coorgi families. This, together with the bare hillsides clothed in mist and the martial bearing of the people, reminded the British planters of Scotland and the Highlands. Even old Dr. K., a Brahmin who had never travelled outside India, recalled how as a child in Mangalore his mother would threaten him with 'The Coorgis are coming, the Coorgis are coming'. Like the Highlanders they specialised in Glencoe-type massacres of any force rash enough to penetrate their hills. They endeared themselves to the British army when this tactic was employed so successfully against the Mysore Sultans in the eighteenth century. In recognition, the Raja of Coorg was presented with a much-prized sword by Lord Wellesley, brother of Wellington of Waterloo.

We arrived in Mercara to find a Coorgi celebration in full swing at the *Kodava Samaj*† headquarters. The Coorgi men were imposingly dressed in hats, like tight square turbans, of white and gold, long black sleeveless coats tied with red and gold sashes, silver watch chains and on one side a small, murderous gold dagger. The Coorgis are a tribe rather than a caste and are thought to be unrelated to any of their immediate neighbours. Their language has been described as a convenient medium for simul-

* Generals 'Timmy' Thimmayya and 'Kipper' Carriappa. Note the nicknames. One can positively smell the pipe smoke of the officer's mess, British style.
† The Coorgi Association. *Kodava* or *Kodaga* is the local name for Coorg.

taneous conversation and betel chewing whilst their physique is said to be stronger and taller than that of the Dravidian. As for the women they too are distinctive. The sari, which in the hands of the washerman is just a length of bright cloth, is normally wound round the body anti-clockwise and drawn up under the right and over the left shoulder. Gujerati women reverse the process by winding clockwise but Coorgi ladies tie both clockwise and back to front. Having wrapped the sari several times round the waist it is usual to collect a bunch of pleats at the front from which the cloth can then be drawn up in a graceful cascading arc across the small of the back under one shoulder and over the other. But the Coorgi ladies gather their pleats at the back. This means a bare midriff and for those who eschew the *choli* (bodice) bare breasts. A handy brooch is introduced to preserve modesty but it destroys the flowing grace of the normal sari. Aside from this peculiarity the Coorgi maidens are famed for their good looks. In a country like India where the beauty and grace of the women is a revelation as staggering as the poverty but less easily ignored this is no mean distinction. It probably has something to do with the emancipated position of women in Coorgi society and with the fact that here there was a settled European community of planters with the leisure to appreciate their surroundings. Or it could be just that, in the effort of stretching for a ripe cluster of coffee beans, that handy brooch is not always entirely dependable.

The Coorgis are nominally Hindus though their pantheon of gods includes a variety of household and nature spirits unknown to the orthodox. In this one is reminded of the Himalayas and the curious deities of Kulu. As we left Mercara the party was still, after several days, in full swing. Something about the music, shrill flutes, a droning bagpipe-like accompaniment and the beat of drums resounding over the hills was again reminiscent of the Himalayas. The thumping, stamping dance of the Coorgi men had nothing in common with the elaborate, formalised Kathakali dancing of Kerala or the graceful posturing of Bharata Natyam, the classical female dance of Tamil Nadu. It was altogether more rumbustuous. That the South should include such an anomalous hill people confirms its claim to be a microcosm of the whole country.

*        *        *

Just as the Ganges rises high in the Himalayas so the Cauvery, the sacred river of the South, rises in the hills of Coorg. It flows south-east past Mysore City, into the Narayan country and so lazily into the rich coastal plain near Trichy and Tanjore. Here one is in a land as hallowed as the Gangetic plain. The orthodoxy, as much as the diversity, of the minority communities of the South is more than matched by that of the Hindu majority. Although it was in the North that the Sanskrit roots of Hinduism spread into the Indian soil much of its subsequent growth has taken place in the South. The famous saints Sankara Acharya, Ramanuja and Madhavacharya to whom can be attributed the prominence of Siva, Vishnu and Krishna in the modern Hindu pantheon were all South Indian Brahmins. Tamil and the other South Indian languages have a richer religious and devotional literature than any other modern Indian tongue. Nowhere in India except perhaps at Benares is the visitor so frequently confronted by the raw faith and devotion of the Indian people. The entire travelling public resplendent with forehead caste marks. as big and gay as fried eggs or raspberry fool seem to be on pilgrimage, heading for a *darshan*, the glimpse of a saint or an *ashram*, a lay monastery.

The vast temple complexes are thronged with people. In the temple at Madurai the offering boxes are giant iron safes embedded in the stone floor. Within its precincts is a bazaar where you can buy pots and pans, baskets, bangles and anklets as well as every conceivable devotional aid—statues, rosaries, joss sticks, bells, oil lamps, flowers and fruits. The air is thick with the smell of jas-

---

* Not to be confused with a *tilaka* or *tikka*, the dab of red paste on the forehead worn by married women. Caste marks are usually sectarian denoting a devotee of Siva or Vishnu rather than the wearer's caste.

mine and bananas and the bright colours of the crowd soon kill the garishly repainted *gopurams* (gateways). In the temple pool devout ladies, always of a certain age, perform that most delicate of *leger de corps*, washing themselves and their saris without the least indecency. Outside there is a building, still part of the temple, where three hundred treadle sewing-machines whirr away beside as many stalls selling silk, cotton and trimmings. In between, a cold-drink stall sells Kali Cola to the faithful. One begins to sense the way in which social life and religion are one. The temple and its religious connotations extend deep into the bazaars just as the bazaars and the gaiety of Indian life extend deep into the temples. With feet accustomed to the smooth warm flagstones of the temple compound one wanders off into the real bazaar, shoes forgotten at the *gopuram*.

If the cities are full of temples the countryside is alive with saints. On a local branch line near Trichy the doctor in our compartment came out with a roll of celebrities for each station along the line. Here lived a man of one hundred and sixty-three who 'passed no water and had no motions'. But if you visited him, and thousands did, you took him food and water. Another man in the carriage joined in but was repeatedly shouted down. They grew quite excited.

'I have seen him eat this food.'

'Ah, yes, but he has spoken to me.'

There were sages who knew and told you the innermost secrets of your life at the first meeting. Others who buried themselves for days—no, months—and re-emerged in the best of health. Further along the line was the saint who liked cigarettes. Not just the cheap Charminar but Wills Filter. One rupee a packet but you always took some because he didn't exhale. The smoke was drawn in but never came out. It was a miracle.

Even G., a far from gullible Oxford graduate, was convinced.

'If you want to see saints you must go to Bangalore. The one really big saint we have today is a person called Satya Sahi Baba. You will remember seeing his portrait. Long hair. That he can perform miracles is beyond question. I mean it. I have met too many people who have had the experience of a sort of saffron coming out of his hands. He just speaks and the saffron comes out. Sometimes jewels as well. You can go there if you like. I don't know where it is, near Bangalore, but I'll find out. Here in Dharwar there was a photograph of him from which the saffron was pouring down. I didn't go because of the crowds. But it was just a photograph belonging to one of his devotees and one day the saffron started to fall. Anyone could go and see, hundreds did.

He is the one genuine saint in India today. There are now swamijis and gurujis who have his photograph. He has become the swami of swamis. The number of people who have become his devotees is quite fantastic. The most famous was an atheistic Kannada writer whose speciality was to lampoon all these swamis. So he went there to lampoon him. Out of a thousand people Satya Sahi Baba picked him out and said 'Now look here, you have such and such problems, your daughter is out of her mind and so on but such and such will happen'. And they did and now he has become one of his greatest devotees. He has become his secretary.

There is another Kannada writer, a very famous novelist, whose wife went mad and wanted to commit suicide. He is an atheist, humanist and so on. She went up to the second floor and wanted to jump when she saw this man, Satya Sahi Baba, who said 'Don't'. So she went down and she recovered. It's a fantastic house to visit because outside this man is sitting and writing or arguing against God and leading a totally non-religious life whilst inside she has a whole room full of photographs of Satya Sahi Baba and has become his great devotee. I didn't believe in miracles but now I think that some people can perform them. But so what?'

We never got to see Satya Sahi Baba though we were increasingly aware of his unique position in India. In Delhi thousands were flocking to his audiences when we next passed through. The newspapers were everywhere taking him seriously and fantastic tales of his powers to produce and distribute diamond necklaces, Swiss watches and gold bars were on everyone's lips. But the comparatively unsensational nature of G'.s stories struck me as far more convincing. And like him the unanswerable question amongst intelligent observers was not whether he could perform these miracles but why. Why was it he needed to attract such publicity by indiscriminate use of powers to which any saint might lay claim if he so wished?

There is no clearer guide to popularity in India than a careful scrutiny of the shops in every bazaar which sell coloured pin-ups of celebrities. In Tamil Nadu Mr. Annadurai is always there, in Bengal Rabindranath Tagore and in Bombay Zoroaster of the Parsis. These local figures compete with the all-Indian celebrities like Mrs. Gandhi and her father Mr. Nehru, the Mahatma and numerous film stars. But even far away in Darjeeling the most popular figure, outselling all, was Satya Sahi Baba. His very Dravidian, almost negroid, features are haloed by an Afro hair style some eight inches deep. He is young and smiling. He wears a red silk night-dress and his eyes are cast down. He could be a soul singer or a pop hero but Indians, normally so critical of exhibitionism, have no reservations where a saint is concerned.

I was particularly delighted with my purchase in Darjeeling; it was a double bill. On one side is a picture of Satya Sahi Baba and on the other another Tamil saint almost as famous but so totally different it is hard to believe they could both be products of the same religious strain. The picture, which is a bad one, is of an old man with spindly legs, a white beard and the kindest of eyes. He is Ramana Maharishi, a saint who lived and died—or rather 'left his body'—on a remote hill in Tamil Nadu, who seldom performed a miracle, seldom even spoke and yet has created a legend which may well survive even Sahi Baba's fame. He was an Ayyar Brahmin who, at the age of eleven, ran away from home to the Arunachala Hill where he spent the rest of his life chiefly in prayer, meditation and fasting.

His teaching was not so very different from that of the great

Bengali revivalist, Ramakrishna, or any of the more recent Westernised versions of Hinduism. Self-realisation is what matters most. Any religion or school of thought which helps one to reach this goal is permissible. In fact self-realisation may well not be an end in itself but simply a means towards an end, towards being a better Catholic, Buddhist or whatever. This at least avoids the embarrassment of would-be converts. It took a fellow swami to convene at Rishikesh in 1953 the 'World Parliament of Religions'. Perhaps to his credit Ramana Maharishi was never so explicit with this eclecticism. His teaching was less influenced by Western thought. It is the simplicity of his life and the peculiar charm of the man which account for his fame. These are remembered not so much by his teaching as by the hill on which he lived. It has, one is told, his 'emanations', and his followers who live in ashrams and private houses at its base are held by its magnetism.

Just as the sociologists and anthropologists are attracted in their droves to India so are the ashramites, the Western disciples of meditation and self-realisation. Meditation is becoming big business and the larger ashrams rival the hotels in their bid to attract the visitor. At Pondicherry the Aurobindo ashram is said to accommodate thousands. The local population claim that none of the accumulated foreign spending power finds its way out of the ashram but business there is so good that Auroville, an international meditational city, is to be built. Here as at other ashrams the *raison d'être* is a saint, the Bengali Aurobindo Ghose, whose handmaiden, the Ma or mother, still lives on. At least she is thought to be 'still in the body' though her appearances in public are rare and far from convincing. And besides to her followers whether she is still 'in the body' or not is irrelevant. Either way she is there.

It is quite normal for these great saints to take a handmaiden or to have one very close female devotee; the Pondicherry Ma is French, Ramana Maharishi's is a distinguished Parsi lady. Even Mahatma Gandhi had his handmaidens but no moral censure is attached to such relationships. Talking to one such Ma I was struck by the sincerity or, if you like, professionalism, of the

Indian saints and gurus. It would be wrong to conclude that the disciples of self-realisation in ashrams from Rishikesh to Rameswaram are all deluded souls in hopeless retreat from Western materialism. The religious leaders of India are highly convincing. They exhibit an honesty, a benign tolerance and understanding comparable to that of Pope John. On the Ma's sitting-room wall hung the Sacred Heart, Zoroaster and her own Hindu saint. She explained with the same smiling simplicity as when talking of life with her own saint, of her meetings with Lord Jesus. Her eyes, radiant with beauty and love, could surely see Christ. And she was obviously overawed by her visions. There was no question of debasing the experience by submitting it to papal scrutiny or scientific investigation. To her they were as real as I was. Anyone who could realise themselves so totally and thus conquer the ego would enjoy the same spiritual experiences. For her it was so very clear and so completely worth while.

I wish one could write as warmly of the Western ashramites. No doubt they are sincere, intelligent seekers of the truth. But what they conspicuously lack is the purity and simplicity of mind which so distinguishes the Indian saint. In many ashrams they undergo great hardship. Two comfortable middle-aged ladies from Brussels—they could so easily have been missionaries—sat down to dinner. The floor was stone and they lowered themselves to a cross-legged position on it. The plates were banana leaves lying limply on the stone, and dinner just rice moistened with pepper water. They eat with the right hand rolling the rice into neat little balls and flicking it into their mouths in the best Indian style. Afterwards they painfully rose and gave their banana leaves to a troop of monkeys waiting hungrily at the door. A pale French girl in a thin blue sari invited them to her cell for Nescafe and they sauntered off talking of powdered milk and a shopping expedition to the bazaar. In the same ashram was Hugo, an immaculately groomed Swiss, and his handsome young disciple. At the 6.20 a.m. milk offering, the equivalent of communion service, I had seen them prostrate on the floor of the main shrine as if cast down there in the exhaustion of some nocturnal religious ecstasy. Hugo's forehead, a wide expanse of flawless ivory complexion, always sported the most perfectly centred and brilliantly coloured *puja* mark. His *kurta*★ and *dhoti* were of a dazzling white and stiff with starch as if in preparation for his first communion. He was a model ashramite and the swami was proud of him. But his eyes were cold and humourless and his voice authoritarian and dry. As soon as we arrived I recognised him as the prototype head boy. And as we slunk out of the ashram grounds for a surreptitious cigarette (shoes and smoking were strictly forbidden) in the nearby mango grove I knew he would loom silent and icily disapproving through the dark foliage.

'You didn't go *there*?' exclaimed a Bangalore friend when we told of the ashram. 'But that's a terrible place. Didn't you know there is a Tantric circle there?'

We didn't. And I must admit we had not noticed anything seriously untoward. But that many Western ashramites in both Hindu and Buddhist establishments look beyond the innocuous syncretism of modern Hinduism seems highly likely. The path of self-realisation is long and tedious, the objective may seem elusive and the possible means towards it are unlimited. If Christianity, even Islam, is acceptable as a way to self-knowledge, so too are more exciting disciplines like Tantricism.

Although Hinduism has no authoritative body to come down on it like a ton of bricks, Tantricism is to orthodox Hindu practice what Black Magic is to Christianity, a cult of the unnatural and the converse with strong erotic overtones. 'Putting this of the female there and eating; taking young girls and eating beef from their this and so on' explained our rather agitated friend. He had a great respect for these Tantric circles. They were not the sort of institutions one dismissed lightly. They were very powerful. Tantricism is almost certainly more discussed than practised but I began to wonder anew about Hugo and his friend. And the pale French girl. Historically Tantricism is associated with the North and Bengal but it was in the Deccan and Tamil Nadu that we were now so often encountering it. Given the religious atmos-

★ The long tunic shirt, usually white, worn all over India.

phere of the South, its variety and intensity, it seemed a likely place for a touch of deviationalism.

Another discipline is yoga. Of this there are many exponents and many schools but with a few exceptions they all assume a relation between spiritual progress along the path of self-knowledge and physical progress along the path of self-discipline. On the fanatical fringe there are exponents who can imbibe through their anus or plug their nostrils—both simultaneously—with their tongue. I doubt whether this is matched by the equivalent in spiritual progress but a more innocent endeavour like the mastery of composure is an obvious aid to meditation. Institutions like the 'Self Realisation Fellowship of the U.S.A.' (incorporating 'The Self-Realisation Church of all Religions', San Diego) founded by Swami Parahamsa Yogananda, owe their success largely to yoga. The disciples at least have something to show for their spiritual exertions.

As sacred as the temples, as booming as the ashrams and as wondrous as the saints is another great religious centre in the south-eastern corner of India. Just in Andhra Pradesh this is the hill shrine of Tirupati, currently the best patronised in India. Pilgrims of the most fanatical persuasion converge on this remote spot from every state in the Union. Even a professed atheist like Mrs. Gandhi visited the shrine four times in a single day amidst a blaze of publicity calculated to swing Hindu votes from the Jan Sangh to the Congress. Normally each party of pilgrims may enjoy *darshan* of the deformed and frightening idol, Lord Venkateswara, for only one minute yet queues still stretch for miles down the hillside and thousands are turned away every night. It is one of the few Hindu shrines so sacred that foreigners are liable to be refused entry. Each day brings a new crop of miracles and the temple authorities enjoy a revenue of astronomical proportions. Besides the beneficence of the faithful they have a booming business in hair which eventually finds its way into the wig shops of London and Paris. Thousands of women shave their heads to enhance a vow or augment a prayer—invariably for a son; Lord Venkateswara likes evidence of the sincerity of supplicants.

## A Madhouse of Religions

Tirupati is one place which Indians seldom debunk. Benares and Puri (Orissa), the more traditional centres of pilgrimage, are often ridiculed as tourist traps full of corrupt ascetics and venal priests but Tirupati is different. It is more exciting, more contemporary and more alive. Like the fame of Satya Sahi Baba or Ramana Maharishi it is the product of ground roots Hinduism, an institution thrown up by the gradual accretion of local folklore and fable, rumour and report, which over the years breaks through the flimsy barriers of credulity, overwhelms the repute of rivals and suddenly breaks forth as a national sensation. For all the talk of a static religion the embers of popular Hinduism are far from dead and nowhere less so than in the South. The battle of Talikota was not such a total disaster. The 'Real India' probably never was but the realities of Hinduism, divisive yet orthodox, pervasive yet tolerant, traditional yet progressive survived the fall of Vijayanagar and the subsequent political integration of the peninsula.

## 5. RUPEES AND REVOLT

## *Western India*

On a warm winter's night in Bihar I was pacing the platform of a small country station waiting for the Kalka Mail to Delhi. The dogs had stopped barking, the porters had disappeared and the numerous peasant families had finished eating and were stretched out on the ground asleep. Sharing my vigil was a young Indian, small with a rich marmite complexion and wearing a blazer. We passed one another several times before finally meeting at the tea stall.

'Excuse me but may I please be knowing your name?'

'John. And yours?'

'Jean-Claud.'

The French accent was faultless. After the endless Singhs and Guptas of the North I could scarcely believe my ears. He came, he explained, from Pondicherry south of Madras, the only size-able remnant of French India to survive into the present century. He was on an All-India Soil Conservation course representing not just 'Pondi' but the whole of the South. It was difficult for him. His colleagues all spoke Hindi or, when showing off, English but he was happier with Tamil or French. Did I by any chance speak French?

Born before 1954 when the French ceded their Indian territory Jean-Claud had the choice of either French or Indian nationality. He had been to Lycée, passed his 'Bachot' and watched many of his friends leave for Paris. He, however, preferred to be Indian. India was now independent and soon with luck he might be Soil Conservation Officer for 'Pondi'.

The more numerous citizens of Goa and the two other small Portuguese ex-colonies on the west coast are not so privileged.

There is no question of their claiming any right to Portuguese nationality. Indian demands for the surrender of what Nehru termed 'these ugly warts on the beautiful face of India' were met by Salazar's total intransigence. Eventually in 1961 India took matters into her own hands and simply annexed the territories. Scarcely a shot was fired; the only casualty was Nehru's much-vaunted policy of peaceful co-existence and this was, anyway, to be finally discredited a few months later in the Himalayan confrontation with the Chinese. Back in Lisbon there are still three Goanese sitting in the national assembly whilst in Goa there are still a few Portuguese expatriates. But the Goanese themselves are not politically minded and even before 1961 were fitting happily into the pattern of minority communities in India proper.

Way back in 1844 in Stocqueveler's Handbook of India their die was already cast. It quotes 'from the graphic pen of Mrs. Postans'. The Goanese 'however offensive he becomes when a ruler, weak as he is as a diplomatist, ridiculous as a beau, ignorant as a priest and useless generally as a member of the native community of India, is yet admirable as a cook . . .; unhappily in this sphere of action his usefulness ends and with it his claims to our attention.' The poor Goanese. In fact they are a well educated, gregarious and predominantly Catholic people with an enviable record of integration. Although invariably bearing Portuguese names and thus referred to as Luso-Indians they are not usually of mixed descent. When a family or village of Goan Indians adopted Christianity they assumed the name of their sponsor or missionary. Thus the legions of Da Souzas, Fernandes and Garcias who today frequent the big cities of India are ethnically as Indian as the rest. As cooks their fame exceeds that of their neighbours to the south at Udipi. In the big new hotels catering for foreigners their Christian lack of taboos on beef and pork are an obvious recommendation. They seem to have acquired a real taste for Western innovations and the entertainment world. Not just the chef but the band and the artistes in any smart restaurant will probably be Goanese. So, too, the pimps will have you believe, are their

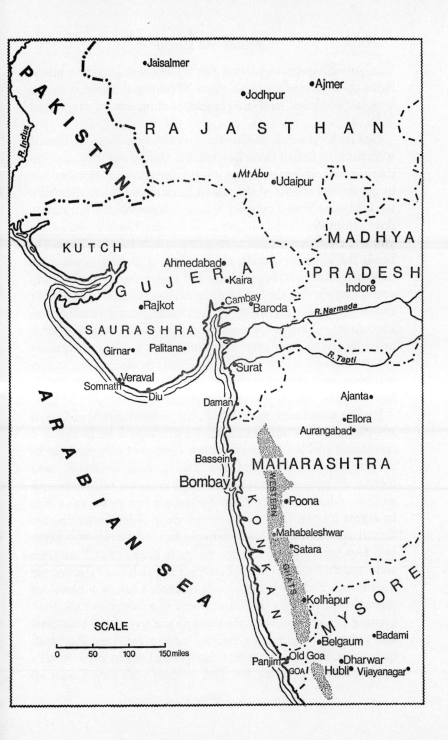

'fair, young, convent-educated girls'. They have become a bright lights caste competing in an effete Westernised idiom with the temple prostitutes and the itinerant musicians of traditional India.

Goa itself now reflects something of this new identity. Blessed with some of India's finest beaches it is rapidly attracting foreign tourist traffic. By air or by sea it is no distance from Bombay but to get the full impact of the place I recommend the approach by road. Mysore State Transport operate a bone-shaking bus service down from Hubli and Belgaum on the dry Deccan plateau. As you trundle down the Western Ghats in a series of tight hairpin bends the air grows moist, then stifling. The jungle, the thick matted African sort, edges nearer and nearer the track. Suddenly you are on the flat, the bus bowling on over sluggish, jungle-clad rivers. Everything is startlingly green with, glimpsed through the vegetation, a shuttered Spanish villa, a vast white baroque church or a village with 'bars' every few yards (drink in Goa is marginally cheaper than elsewhere in India and readily available). The impact is tremendous; after the parched austerity of the Deccan all this luxuriance of colours and associations.

Panjim, sometimes called Panaji, the modern capital of Goa, is straight out of Graham Greene. Scobie would be living in a crumbling villa looking out through a grove of palm trees on to the lazy Rio Mandovi. Just below, two crowded ferries cross and recross, dodging the dhows which drift in on the tide laden with sardines, pomfret and herrings. The jungle laps round the town. In a year or two it could take over the tree-lined avenues, the formal squares and the bland baroque façades as easily as it has in Old Goa where you watch for snakes in the nave of Bom Jesus and fight through the matted creepers to reach the Palace of the Inquisition. Perhaps it has already started. Grass is pushing up through the Avenida da Brasil where the Grandees took their evening stroll. Small boys pee through the river front balustrade and pungent little fish crushed by pedestrians litter the broad pavements. Past the shuttered, ochre-painted stucco villas moves a motley crowd, beaming Konkani women with saris drawn up round their waists, their arms thick with bangles and fish baskets on their heads, gaggles of mini-skirted convent girls and perhaps a pale, perspiring nun, a bony, half-naked saddhu or a bedraggled hippy. On the evening menu at the Hotel Mandovi there's wild boar curry and roast beef with dancing to the Lisbon hit parade sung by three mulatto girls in tight sequined dresses. Mysoreans and Maharashtrans talk of going to Goa as a considerable and slightly naughty adventure. It still owes more to Vasco da Gama, Albuquerque and Francis Xavier than to any one Indian. But then so does Pondicherry to Dupleix and Simla to the Viceroys. Sensibly the Indian government has not tried to force Goa into one of the neighbouring states or impose too many pan-Indian institutions. It remains a Union Territory administered direct by the central government in Delhi.

It was a source of comfort to the Indian government that even before 1961 there were more Goanese in Bombay than in Goa. Bombay gives this impression about all the peoples of western India. With the exception of Calcutta no city so dominates its hinterland. Western India, that is the states of Gujerat and Maharashtra, roughly corresponds to the Bombay Presidency of British times. Historically there is little else to connect the Rajput princelings of Saurashtra, the Muslim kings of Gujerat, the trading powers along the coast and the Mahratta princes behind the Western Ghats. But to the whole region the city of Bombay has now given its own special character. It is, above all, the business capital of India, a city brazenly devoted to the making, hoarding and occasional spending of money. Calcutta has its mills and factories, Delhi its secretariats and embassies and Bombay its banks and business houses. Western India was always comparatively prosperous but the growth of Bombay both attracted the mercantile communities of the area and canalised its trade. The ports of Bassein, Surat, Cambay and Veraval lost out to the expanding metropolis; it became the real Gateway of India, its portals open not just to foreign rulers but to techniques and ideas imported from the West. Here there are more tall buildings, more long cars and more tight trousers than anywhere else in India. It is the centre of the Indian film industry, second in turnover only to that of the U.S.A., and the goal of every restless Indian school-boy.

The streets, however, are not paved with gold, but cluttered with reclining bodies; and the men who build the fancy sky-scrapers for Air India and Indianoil are themselves living in huts of straw and beaten-out tins in what will soon be the car park. Driving in from the airport you pass miles of shanty town where land in the process of reclamation is covered with tumble-down shacks before it is even drained. And even the drainage pipes before they are sunk in the marshy soil provide accommodation for a few hundred more families. Life in a pipe, the open ends blocked with sacking or rush matting, the floor levelled in places with mud and planks—is this the best India's richest city can do for its residents?

Of course nothing in India is as simple as that. For one thing Bombay is critically overcrowded. Unlike Calcutta it can't just sprawl. When the area was sold to the East India Company by Charles II—it had come along with Tangier as part of the dowry of his queen, Catherine of Braganza—it consisted of a lot of pesti-lential islands with a few coco-nut palms and a large fishing com-munity. The ground rent was £10 per annum. The effect of its development into fort, port and city has been to join up these islands, reclaiming the land from the sea where possible and throwing viaducts across where not. The fishermen are still there; on the same road from the airport you pass one of their muddy creeks jammed with masts and rigging. Stuck in the middle of a piece of typically Indian suburbia it's like stumbling on a cattle market in the middle of Hounslow. The city is spreading too fast. Land reclamation lags behind while the city gobbles up creeks and islands which, left alone, might have relieved its hideous monotony and given the planners a chance.

Then there is the shape of Bombay. It hangs like a drooping claw about to pick at the Konkan coast. The wrist is so narrow and marshy that there are only two roads out of the city. Both are appallingly congested but most of the city's expansion is taking place to the north on what is in fact yet another island. The men working on the downtown skyscrapers would certainly object to living out there; it's much too far to walk and what Indian labourer has ever been able to afford transport or contractor willing to supply it? A further complication is that like so much of Bombay's population the labourers do not really belong here. When the monsoon comes in June most of them move off to their villages in the Deccan. Why should anyone bother about housing for those who are not permanent residents?

'To know her is to love her,' says the Bombay sight-seers' brochure. 'To see her once is to want to see her again and again. Some call her heartless. They forget how she opens her heart to the thousands who flock to her with their dreams. Some call her proud. They forget that never does she deny sanctuary to even the humblest among the humble.'

And so on. Fascinated by this punchy copy we emerged from the crisp air-conditioning, the silent lifts and the plush foyer of the State Tourist Office into a blazing, taxi-less afternoon. Across the road a girl of about sixteen was picking her way barefoot through a maze of shimmering reinforced concrete blocks. On her head was a boulder steadied with one hand, on her hip a baby steadied with the other. The baby was howling, the girl was swaying; for both the abyss was yawning. I should have felt sick. Or angry. Or at least sad. In fact I just cursed the dearth of taxis. It is difficult to explain how easy it is to take scenes like that for granted. Only when the girl falls, or when a heavy shower has just flooded out the pipe dwellers does the misery of it all suddenly strike home again. And even then it is horror at one's own callousness rather than sympathy for the weak and homeless which hits one hardest. It is tempting to criticise the wealthy socialites in their air-conditioned apartments on Malabar Hill, the Mayfair of Bombay, to wonder how they manage to square their social consciences in the presence of such abject poverty and hardship, but only a short experience of the Indian dilemma will provide an answer. A mal-nourished child, a tramp suffering from exposure, or an old hag drinking meths stops you dead in the streets of Paris or London. But in India poverty is the norm. You are stunned by it, you accept it, you cease to notice it. The Bombay film star surrounded by sycophantic disciples or the businessman pursuing the necessary import licence for his new Chevrolet simply does not notice. Every day in India the sun shines. You stop opening conversations with a breezy "Nother lovely day'. Soon you notice only the clouds as they gather for the annual rains. The presence of the sun you have taken for granted—just so with poverty.

★    ★    ★

Besides its luxurious apartment blocks the Malabar Hill area of Bombay is famous for its Parsi gardens in which stand the Towers of Silence. Here the urbane Parsi tycoon who now entertains his guests with imported whisky at eight pounds a bottle and dresses in silk shirts and Harris tweed, will soon end his days, a pale naked body fought over by a huddle of heavy hunched vultures and sleek ravenous crows. Here, too, will come Dara and Dilly, the young Parsi couple in Bangalore who, in shorts and climbing boots, played the guitar and sang the whole of 'Ilkley Moor Bar 'tat' in best youth hostel style. Or the secretary of the Old British Club in Mahabaleshwar with his walking stick and tweed-skirted wife. They are all so European, so reassuringly familiar, that one must look again at the Towers of Silence to dispel the illusion. The vultures rouse themselves as the funeral procession approaches, following its progress, observing the last rites. The body is carried into the open arena of the Tower—it is not tall, more like a small open stadium. The floor slopes towards a hole in the centre down which the cleaned bones will eventually be washed. If the corpse is a man he will be placed in the outermost ring of shallow compartments, a woman in the centre and a child in the innermost ring. Everything is of marble or granite, grooved and sloped for easy cleaning. The corpse bearers retreat and the birds circle lower, alight and eat. In the few descriptions of the

Towers one is reminded of the frightening ingenuity of the Nazi gas chambers. To a Western way of thinking the whole procedure is not so much revolting as simply inhuman.

Parsi means Persian. It was from Persia that the first Zoroastrian refugees, fleeing Mohammedan persecution, came to Gujerat and much later, fleeing from further persecution, to Bombay. With them they brought the sacred fire kindled by their prophet, Zoroaster, in the sixth century B.C., symbol of one of the world's most exclusive religions. God is in everything so that the earth, the air, fire and water are sacred. A corpse burning on the banks of the Ganges defiles all four but in the Towers of Silence only the vultures are defiled.

Into Hindu society the Parsis fitted easily. Not only do Parsis never proselytise but they seldom even talk of their religion. Conversion is impossible and the fire temples are closed to all non-believers. Appropriately there is one opposite the American Express for no community is quite so closely identified with money and big business. To a large extent the commercial pre-eminence of Bombay is their creation. In Gujerat their women adopted the sari as the price of acceptance; in Bombay it was the tweed skirt and pearl necklace. In the ultimate gesture of loyalty to the British they even took up cricket. The Parsi financier who, as Victorian tradesman and moneylender 'wore a tall shiny black hat', is now more typically British than some of his young Oxford-educated executives. Amongst the 'native' communities of India the Parsis were accorded pride of place as a civilised, emancipated and highly educated people. Their charitable foundations shamed the Christian missions and their urban pride excelled that of the London merchants. Even their skin and features were of a paler, more European type. Traditional Parsi names like Irani, Masani, Cama and Tata were augmented with more descriptive titles like Readymoney for a moneylender or Bottlewallah (corrupted to Batlavala) for a liquor merchant. Admiration for their overlords or simply the desire of the tradesman to keep in with his customers even led to a few Parsi 'Curzons' and 'Willingdons'. A more typical and traditional name is that of the greatest Parsi bene-

factor and the first Indian baronet Sir Jamshedjee Jeejeebhoy.\*
Or, today, the commander of India's armed forces, Field-Marshal
Sam Hormusji Framji Jamshedji Manekshaw.

Outside Bombay small Parsi communities are found in most
of the major cities, in the coastal towns of the west and, following
the pattern of their British customers, in the hill stations of Darjeeling, Simla, Mount Abu and Mahabaleshwar. From the liquor
and tinned food business they graduated into the management of
hotels. There is no cosier place than a Parsi hotel. The photograph
of a bearded Zoroaster hangs over the mantelpiece, the armchairs
are covered with chintz and the food is strictly European. Ping-
pong and billiards, a couple of dozy spaniels and a garden full of
struggling roses and parched lawn complete the scene. Between
the chink of tea cups one may hear a murmured nostalgia for the
good old days. Things for the Parsi are not what they were.
There is, of course, the Tata family whose business interests are
so vast that they may or may not be running the country. But
for the orthodox the fact that Firoz Gandhi, the prime minister's
husband, was a Parsi is cause for regret rather than congratulation.
Too many good Parsis are marrying outside the community. Even
at the Towers of Silence all is not well. There is a critical shortage
of corpse bearers and no class of impoverished Parsis from
which to recruit more. Wealth and *élitism* have brought their
own problems which threaten to succeed where persecution failed.

At one time running a close second to the Parsis as Bombay's
most enlightened community were the Khojas. They too first
arrived as refugees from Persia. They were Muslims of the Ismaili
sect, followers of a religious leader claiming direct descent from
Mohammed and now known as the Aga Khan. Western India
already had a lively and successful Khoja community when, in
1845, the Aga Khan himself reached Bombay. The horsemen,
eight hundred or so, who accompanied him were all said to be
his sons. There ensued decades of argument and litigation between
the old and the new arrivals but business was good and the Aga

---

\* Parsi names often include a number of '-ji's or '-jee's. They are not to be confused
with '-ji' as a suffix denoting respect or affection.

Khans acquired enormous wealth together with a reputation for charitable works which rivals that of Sir Jamshedjee Jeejeebhoy. To the Ismaili Khoja the Aga Khan is both the supreme spiritual and temporal ruler. This authority, like that of India's other god-like refugee the Dalai Lama, is paramount and includes the right to tax his followers. After nearly a hundred years of residence in Bombay the Aga Khans re-emerged not just as kings and prophets but also as the sect's supreme bankers. The city can claim to have spawned one of the world's greatest financial empires and to have turned a harassed and fanatical Persian sect into a boardroom brotherhood.

Just what happened to the Khojas of Bombay remains, to me, a mystery. Aga Khan III was the first to visit Europe and start the tradition of an international, jet-setting, horse-racing family. Many Khojas undoubtedly followed his example and sizeable communities are now found in Europe, America and East Africa as well as Pakistan. At the time of India's partition more no doubt moved to Africa or to Pakistan. But in Bombay there must still be at least a small colony. Inquiries only lead to the main communities of Sunni and Shiah Muslims living in well-defined areas near the Crawford Market or off Colaba Road. But if they have really withdrawn from the rat race of Bombay commerce there is no shortage of successors. Just as Delhi opened its arms to the Sikhs fleeing from Lahore in 1947 so Bombay welcomed the Hindu Sindhis from Karachi. Here in the west the movement of Muslims to Pakistan and Hindus to India was on nothing like the scale of the migrations in the north but amongst the more prosperous classes it was still considerable. The Sindhis are now a very influential body in the business network of the west.

All these refugee people along with the considerable foreign business community could scarcely have made Bombay what it is were it not for the mercantile classes and castes of the native population of western India. As Marwaris, Gujeratis, Jains or Banias they are seldom differentiated though all these terms are far from synonymous. The role of the trader and moneylender is enshrined in the caste system and Hindu tradition. Indians are not wholly the saintly, other-worldly people one is often lead to believe. The accumulation of gold, jewellery and rupees is a national obsession which, by drawing so much currency out of circulation, paralyses the economy. Even the illiterate peasant has an astounding grasp of compound interest and an often touching respect for figures and currency.

'What is the name of your village?' inquired a bent old man who had joined us at the tea shop in a forgotten little village of the Deccan.

'London.'

'How much money does it cost to come from London to this village?'

'A lot of money.'

'But how much?'

'Six, seven hundred rupees.' He smiled and spoke to the old lady who owned the tea shop.

'It must be more.' I tried again to work it out.

'Oh, six to seven thousand rupees. But that's return.' He nodded seriously. Now I was talking. That was real money. Respectfully he discussed the figure with the old lady and passed the news on to the two men who sat on their haunches in the dusty track to watch us.

'Is it nearer six or seven thousand?'

Could this sort of money mean anything to these people, I wondered. A cup of tea cost fifteen *paise*,\* a flat bun twenty *paise*, a meal perhaps one rupee and a chicken, if the village possessed any, perhaps seven rupees. The bus for which we were waiting was a long time coming. A crowd of villagers returning from the fields joined us; more arrived to wait for the bus. By the time it came the whole price structure of international air travel had been reviewed. Although no one had actually been as far as Bombay they all knew the fare to the nearest *paise* and quickly converted it for me into sterling when furnished with the current exchange rate.

\* There are one hundred *paise* or *nai paise* (NP) to a rupee (R). The current exchange rate is about seven rupees to the dollar or eighteen to the pound.

In traditional village society the money-lender is as much part of the scene as the local landowner, the village idiot, the troupe of monkeys and the peepul tree under which you pass the time of day. Everyone, including the landowner, is in his debt and paying exorbitant rates of interest. He is universally disliked and invariably caricatured as a plump greasy fellow with small soft hands and a grossly falsified ledger. He wears a long coat and ties his turban in distinctive fashion. His caste is that of the dreaded Bania. Why the money-lending Bania has become so closely identified with Marwar, the old name for Jodhpur state in Rajasthan, is not clear. But just as Brahmin cooks invariably come from Udipi or *dhobis* (washermen) from U.P., so money-lenders and successful merchants of Bania caste come from the desert cities of Rajasthan, from Bikaner, Jaipur, Ajmer and Jodhpur. Many still ply their trade round the villages but in the cities, Calcutta as much as Bombay, they have attained an almost incredible degree of influence, wealth and respectability. The Birla family, whose trading interests rival those of the Parsi Tatas, represent the peak of such achievement.

Also closely identified with Rajasthan but even more so with Gujerat are the Jains. They are neither a caste nor a regional group but a religious sect. They may well be both Marwaris and of Bania descent. In Delhi not far from the Red Fort there's a building proclaiming itself as 'Birds Hospital'. I used to feel a little sorry for the charitable Mr. or Dr. Bird whose foundation sounded like a home for orphaned mynahs and rheumatic peacocks. But this is India and that, precisely, is what it is; a Jain sanatorium for birds. In Ahmedabad, the Jain metropolis in Gujerat, there are big stone bird tables on the street corners and boarding houses where you can stay free of charge on one condition, that you slaughter neither flea nor mosquito. The Jain's respect for life in all its forms is nothing short of an obsession. In a delightful hotel in Mysore City run by a smiling young Jain, the mosquito netting was so thick that even cigarette smoke could not penetrate it. There was to be no excuse for the habitual, last-thing-at-night massacre.

In this reverence for life and the strict vegetarianism which it enjoins one is reminded of Buddhism and of Ashoka's injunctions. In fact the Jain founder, Mahavira, was a contemporary of the Buddha and also lived and taught in Bihar in the sixth century B.C. The religion he founded was largely monastic and along with Buddhism swept over the subcontinent at the beginning of the Christian era. Jain caves are found along with Buddhist caves at Ellora in Maharashtra and with Brahmin caves at Badami in Mysore. The Brahmin revival in the sixth to ninth centuries which virtually wiped out Buddhism—or at least re-absorbed it— in the whole of India was less fatal to Jainism. The Jains were only monks. They could accept Brahmin authority and their lay followers could continue to observe the caste system without prejudice to the asceticism and metaphysics of their system. Even today it is not always clear whether a Jain layman is regarded as anything other than a Hindu and Jainism as anything other than a Hindu sect.

In dress and appearance the laity have few peculiarities. Only after visiting a few Jain caves and temples does one begin to sense the vastly different cultural tradition. At Badami you climb away from the town and from the troupe of monkeys and screaming children ('Whattis yor nem, whattis yor nem?') to three caves full of squirming gods and cavorting goddesses. Gyrating groups all arms, legs and wasp waists denote the true Hindu tradition of interfering and distracting deities. A few yards on there's a fourth cave. It has much the best position with a view not over the humming little town below, but over a peaceful lake to the distant slopes. Looking impassively out from the veranda is an unmistakably Jain figure. He stands naked and to attention. Not even a Greek god could look so unmoving. Thighs and pectorals, shoulders and genitals, all are exactly as they should be in perfect proportion. The same motionless figures are found in every Jain shrine and temple from Gwalior and Parasnath (Madhya Pradesh and Bihar) to Mangalore (Mysore). Sitting cross-legged like a Buddha, standing bolt upright or, very occasionally, lying down, they are always the same, masculine, solid, expressionless, lifeless.

But before dismissing the Jains as totally unfeeling and humour-less you should also see Mount Abu or one of the other Jain centres in western India. At Abu the children are all shouting 'Good after', good after'' (the temples are open to visitors only in the afternoon). You enter the complex with no foretaste of what is in store. The *sikharas* (towers) are very ordinary and the stone of the exteriors is a dull grey. The date is about A.D. 1100. Back in England they were marvelling at the Norman arch. Most of Florence was still a swamp. You shed your shoes, belt, watch-strap and anything else that might be leather—Jains are even more paranoiac about cows than Hindus—and enter the first temple. It's like, on a more intimate scale, the Taj Mahal. The whole of the interior, floor, walls and the roof of the central shrine, is white marble. The bright sunlight is seemingly trapped between so many dazzling surfaces and the sky seen through white marble pillars looks indigo. Eyes slowly grow accustomed to the glare and you notice a piece of delicate carving on the capitals, then more on the *Mandapam* and on the porch. The whole place is carved, as intricately and elaborately as an ivory trinket. Only the floor is smooth, impossibly smooth, as your bare feet slide happily over it. You experience a sense of weightlessness. Unlike a Hindu temple the whole place is spotlessly clean; there are no greasy lingams, no slippery puddles of *ghi*. And the priests are not the wild-looking *purohits** of Madurai but vaguely ethereal figures gliding noiselessly round the fifty-two outer shrines. In each of these sits a solitary *Jina*, more a prophet or 'great spirit' than a god. To any but a Jain they are indistinguishable except for variations in the marble. Some have eyes of black marble, some faces of black marble with eyes of white. Great prominence is also given to nipples and belly buttons; at the modern Hathi Singh temple in Ahmedabad they are picked out in what looks like silver paper.

The other distinctive feature of Jain shrines is their positioning. Abu, Parasnath (Bihar), Palitana and Girnar (Gujerat) are all con-siderable hills commanding extensive views of the surrounding

---

* Temple priests. In the South they shave the front of the head but let the hair grow long from the back.

countryside. At Parasnath the Calcutta Jains, mostly Marwari businessmen, are carried up the 3,000 feet sitting cross-legged like their Jina on a little canopied swing suspended from a long pole with a porter at each end. It seemed a curious way of going on pilgrimage but the Jain businessman is seldom an athletic figure. The base of the hill and each of its peaks and buttresses is scattered with well-kept white temples. A network of paths clinging to the cliff's edge connects them. The Jain pilgrim looks out from his swing on to the peaceful world of nature and sees that it is good. The businessman finds in his religion a perfect antidote to the rat race and the stock market.

The year 1974 is being celebrated as the 2,500th anniversary of Mahavira's death. The *Times of India* reported that 'Among suggestions for the celebrations are convening a world peace conference in 1974, declaring 1974 as world peace year and closing all slaughter houses at least on Lord Mahavira's birthday. . . . One of the Jain *munis* (monks) walked stark naked into Parliament House where the meeting was held.' An extension of the Jain reverence for life is the doctrine of 'ahimsa' adopted and translated by Mahatma Gandhi into the creed of 'non-violence' and hence of world peace. The naked *muni*, a member of the Digambara or 'sky-clad' sect of Jains exemplifies the same doctrine. Digambaras forgo clothing for fear that wearing it they may crush an insect in its folds. The other sect of Jain monks, the Svetambara, wear clothes, usually white, but cover their mouths with a gauze mask to discourage flies from an untimely death between the mandibles. And they sweep the ground ahead of them for fear of squashing an innocent ant or a sleeping scorpion. In Jaipur Svetambara are a common sight but the naked Digambara, looking as aloof and unself-conscious as Jinas, usually stick to the centres of pilgrimage.

Ahmedabad (Gujerat) with a population of over a million, is traditionally the centre of the colossal Indian textile business in which the Jains have a considerable interest. Here their charitable reputation, as great as that of the Parsis or Khojas, is well evidenced in schools and homes for sick animals. The Abu temples suggest the wealth of the Jains eight hundred years ago. And just as Bombay is the product of British and Parsi acumen so Ahmedabad is of the Jains. It's a chaotic sort of city; the narrow streets are choked with the exhaust fumes of noisy motor rickshaws and the architecture is a hopeless jumble of Hindu, Muslim and Art Deco styles. There is only one Western-style hotel, the Cama— presumably a Parsi encroachment. Otherwise it's all very Indian and somehow preferable to Bombay. Bombay, too, has a vast textile business, a considerable Jain presence and a lot of very Indian architecture, but there is also that pervading Western façade which makes its poverty more striking and its callousness more offensive. A shack, two of whose walls are billboards advertising soft drinks and washing machines, is decidedly worse than one with walls made out of unadorned packing cases. And a city where the waterfront is an insalubrious prospect of rubbish-choked riverbed is in India somehow better than one where the vista is of jaunty sailing dinghies heaving alongside a spotlit dance floor projecting into the turquoise Arabian Sea.

*    *    *

Back in Bombay and not far from the bobbing dance floor stands the Taj Mahal Hotel, as famous almost as the Taj Mahal itself, and before it the Gateway of India, a vast stone archway erected to receive the King-Emperor George V. As if challenging this ponderous structure a fine statue of a horse and rider faces it from beside the hotel. The horse is rampant and the rider wears a tasselled night cap and is brandishing his sword. The Indian tourists who give the Gateway only a casual glance stand entranced before this horseman. The statue was erected only in 1960 but horse and rider have more right here than the Gateway. For this is Sivaji* the Great, founder of Mahratta power and India's hero extraordinary. Ask any Indian schoolboy who was the most famous figure in Indian history and he will reply unhesitatingly Sivaji. He constructed no empire, founded no dynasty and won

---

* No connection with the god Siva, though given the respectful '-ji' he too appears as Sivaji.

not a single pitched battle but to India he is Napoleon. Only Mahatma Gandhi can rival the contemporary reverence in which he is held though two more dissimilar founder fathers it is difficult to imagine.

Until 1960 Bombay was the capital of Bombay state, previously the Bombay Presidency. In that year serious rioting over the inevitable language issue—Gujerati versus Marathi—led to the partitioning of the state into Gujerat and Maharashtra. Behind the language issue lay a deeper division. Gujeratis are a peaceful trading and dairy-farming people imbued with traditional Hindu and Jain ethics. Gujerati shopkeepers are found all over the Pacific and East Africa while close links with the Arab world made the ports of Saurashtra the busiest in India. Mahrattas on the other hand are a militant race, horsemen and hill farmers rather than cowherds and merchants, with their own rugged kind of Hinduism. Though Bombay is now the capital of Maharashtra you must go up through the moist western slopes of the Ghats to the dry, rocky sierras behind to see the Mahratta on his own home ground. From Poona south to Belgaum in Mysore the land is stark and hostile. Even the torrential monsoon rains, up to four hundred inches in some places, which pour down these rocky slopes and jagged cliffs create only rivulets of fertile soil in the deep ravines; the hills are scarred not mellowed by their progress. In the towns and villages the wiry Mahratta people are untouched by the Westernising antics of Bombay. Milling through the crowd at a village fair near Satara I was head and shoulders above a sea of dazzling headgear. Everyone wore the traditional Hindu turban loosely tied with a long tail hanging down the back; the colours were of brilliant crimson, deep orange and a startling pale yellow. Occasionally I glimpsed an upturned face as gnarled as the roots of a banyan or, protruding from the precarious turban, an enormous ear sporting long black hairs like the growth on a buffalo's cheek.

These are the men who erupted under the leadership of Sivaji and subsequent Mahratta princes to terrorise the Moghul empire during the seventeeth and eighteenth centuries. They were not

novices in the art of war. The local Chalukyan empire of the
fifth century A.D. had probably relied on Mahratta troops as did
the Bahmanid kingdom which contested control of the Deccan
with the Vijayanagar empire in the fifteenth century. But an
improvement in the quantity and breed of horses as a result of
Muslim imports from Arabia and a general decay in the armed
forces of the Moghul empire together with the political instability
of the Deccan in the late seventeenth century gave the Mahrattas
their chance. All they needed was a leader and for once history
produced the man for the moment. Sivaji was the son of a local
baron, a Sudra by caste but a man who both respected Hindu
tradition and knew how to exploit it. Posing as the liberator of
the Hindu majority from the yoke of Muslim rule he led his
army of Mahratta horsemen from Gujerat to Hyderabad and
Tanjore. They were the fastest, most elusive troops India had
ever seen. According to the Cambridge History of India the
Mahratta horseman carried just his arms, a blanket, a flap of
bread and the occasional onion. He relied not on heavy baggage
trains and herds of camp followers but on plunder and protection
money. Against the imperial artillery, elephants and infantry he
would have fared badly in a pitched battle. Sivaji appreciated this.
Perpetual harassment with an eye to plunder and the eventual
capitulation of the enemy was the main tactic. It brought sensational results. In twenty years of restless campaigning Sivaji con-
solidated his position in the Western Ghats, acquiring a vast slice
of the Deccan stretching diagonally across the peninsula and held
together by a chain of impressive fortresses. He kept the cream
of the Moghul army tied up in the Deccan and made the most
powerful empire India had ever known look ridiculous.

Much has been made of Sivaji's personal defiance of Aurangzeb
and his emissaries. His career started with his refusal to join the
emperor for a campaign in the Deccan. He inveigled the commander of the forces sent to punish him for this omission into a
personal interview. They met unarmed but Sivaji had fitted on to
his hand a pair of lethal claws with which he swiftly disembowelled
the other. The claws, along with *Jai Bhawani*, the great man's

sword, and other bits of Sivajiana may be seen by the persevering visitor in Satara. There is a museum but the real weapons are enshrined in what is more like a temple with the sword reposing in an inner sanctum guarded by a priest and surrounded by oil lamps and dead flowers, evidence of a recent *puja*. Later Sivaji was brought to Aurangzeb's court and offered the command of five thousand horse; the Moghul armies were full of Rajput generals who had been won over in this way. Sivaji was so incensed he fainted. He was then arrested but escaped in disguise. Exploits such as these are well documented and have supplied the Bombay film industry with not a few themes. But the market for movies about Sivaji is virtually inexhaustible. Several 'Easterns' have been made with Mahrattas instead of cowboys or indians. Robin Hood was too good to miss and sure enough the Merry Men with Sivaji as Robin and a jolly Brahmin as Friar Tuck sallied forth from their parched strongholds in the treeless ghats to waylay Aurangzeb, the Sheriff of Nottingham.

Histories talk of the 'robber prince' and Aurangzeb called him the 'desert rat' but nowadays Sivaji is credited with a good deal more than adventure. His administration was well planned and highly effective. As Peshwas or chief ministers he appointed Brahmins but the rest of the system was based on the best local example, that of the extinct Bahmanid empire. Against the Muslim enemy no tactic was too underhand and no torture too brutal. He saw himself as the founder of a Hindu state and the leader of a resurgent, militant Hinduism. It was the beginning of the last great Hindu–Muslim confrontation, one which restored the self-confidence of a nation before the establishment of British rule finally blew the whistle on six hundred years of intermittent Hindu–Muslim warfare.

The Hindu state which Sivaji envisaged never materialised but the military power of the Mahrattas continued to control or terrorise an ever-increasing section of the subcontinent. Mahratta armies penetrated as far even as Bengal and Punjab. Sivaji's successor was the Mahratta Confederacy in which five great houses were dominant. These were, from Gujerat the Gaikwars of Baroda, from the north of Madhya Pradesh the Scindias of Gwalior, from central India the Bhonslas of Nagpur and the Holkas of Indore, and from the Mahratta homeland the Peshwas of Poona. All except the last continued to represent militant Hindu regionalism well into the nineteenth century and to rely heavily on the horsemen and tactics bequeathed by Sivaji. But against the doddering and dissipated puppets who succeeded Aurangzeb on the Imperial throne their task was a good deal easier. Though checked in 1760 by the Afghan invaders who shored up the Moghul throne it took the disciplined armies and superior weaponry of the British to destroy Mahratta power for good.

Especially noteworthy is the confederate structure of Mahratta power. Right from the time of the Mahabharata this type of loose association of great houses with a strong regional base seems to have fitted the Hindu genius better than a monolithic empire on the Moghul pattern. The Rajput princes exemplified the same system and even the Vijayanagar empire was closer to a confederation than an empire in the European sense. Sivaji's successors recognised what today is enshrined in the federal nature of India's Constitution. What united these confederacies, Rajput, Vijayanagar and Mahratta, was the threat of Muslim arms and their own shared allegiance to Hindu tradition. Once the threat subsided they were never averse to fighting amongst themselves. But when it reappeared it was on the basis of shared loyalty to the Vedas or the example of Krishna* that concord was forged. A modern parallel is the cohesion which independent India derives from the existence, supposed or real, of the militant Islamic threat posed by Pakistan. It has even been suggested that this threat is regarded as a necessity for the survival of a united India.

\*    \*    \*

Given a few hours at Bombay airport—in this, at least, Indian Airlines seldom disappoint—one begins to notice the prevalence

* In the Mahabharata.

of a particular type of Indian. He is there amongst the gaggle of excited nuns waiting for their flight to Cochin and there again, only in greater force, behind a party of full blown Indian matrons, their nylon saris tied in Gujerati style and billowing like spinnakers as they bear down on the jet to Baroda. There are even one or two waiting in the minuscule little plane which should have left for Rajkot three hours ago. They are all middle-aged, all dressed in white and all, though surrounded by friends, seem to be looking for someone else. On their heads are white cotton hats called Nehru or Gandhi caps which are much like those worn by American sailors. And on their feet brown lace-up shoes and socks project incongruously from the lowest fold of a *dhoti*. A long white coat with high collar and buttons from neck to waist is preferred to the simple *kurta* if the weather permits. The whole outfit is made of cotton, supposedly homespun, and called *khaddi*. This is important for these men are the would-be successors of Mahatma Gandhi and Pandit Nehru. They wear white *khaddi*, they will tell you, because it was the symbol of protest in the struggle for independence. Did not Mahatmaji say that India must spin for freedom and so eliminate the market for Lancashire cotton goods? Many of them may be businessmen, doctors or lawyers anxious to assert their political awareness. But some will be politicians and for them whatever their party this outfit is *de rigueur*. Even Communist M.P.s like to associate themselves with the independence struggle. In western India it is the Congress Party which still predominates. Here the men in *khaddi* are the true Congress-wallahs, the archetype of every Indian politician.

Nowhere in India is the Congress-wallah* so much in evidence. In his person the various themes of western India, Jain asceticism and the belief in *ahimsa*, the Mahratta tradition of Hindu militancy and the universal obsession with trade and money are strangely, even conflictingly, united. The independence movement was financed by the big business houses of Bombay. Subhas

---

* A taxi-wallah drives a taxi, a rickshaw-wallah pulls a rickshaw and so on. Everyone is a wallah of some sort. 'Fellow' would be the nearest English equivalent.

Chandra Bose, the Bengali independence leader, was nicknamed Netaji like Sivaji's master of the horse. Gandhi himself was a Gujerati from Porbandar in Saurashtra.\* Outside his old school in Rajkot there is a statue of him with a pair of round Gandhi spectacles kindly supplied by the local optician who made the original ones. The textile industry of Ahmedabad spearheaded the *khaddi* business and the great salt march led by Gandhi in protest against a tax on Indian salt was held in Gujerat. Two other great architects of independence, Sardar Vallabhai Patel who secured the integration of the princely states and Morarji Desai, the exponent of non-violence and prohibition—Gandhi's successor in the ascetic tradition—were Gujeratis. In the long struggle western India's contribution was the greatest and even today one is not allowed to forget it.

To his traditional themes the Congress-wallah has added a few imported ideas. Of these socialism is the one about which one hears most. India is a socialist republic, Congress stands for secularism and socialism. Gandhi fought for the abolition of caste and social justice for the outcastes. Nehru was a left-wing intellectual, a Fabian, and had close connections with the British Socialist Party. For the Congress Party of Mrs. Gandhi socialism means the betterment of people's economic lot by the nationalisation of all important industries, the reduction of all large landholdings, the removal of privilege from those like the princes and capitalists who have enjoyed it. What then, one might ask, of those incredibly wealthy Birlas and Tatas in their Bombay skyscrapers? How is it they still both survive and prosper? How can you talk of socialism when major industries like the airlines, the manufacture of cars and trucks, and the press are controlled by just four or five big family empires? Not only do these families continue in the best, or worst, capitalist tradition but the ruling Congress Party owes more than it likes to admit to their support, moral and otherwise.

If this is all a little shocking how about standards of political

\* His family were of Bania caste. Though not Jains they would have been influenced by the Jain presence in Saurashtra.

morality? Gujerat is a very traditional state with an unbroken history of Congress rule. In the five-year period of 1967–72 two-thirds of the state M.L.A.s (equivalents of the national M.P.s) changed their party allegiance; one stalwart switched five times in this period. The incentives, it is candidly admitted, were bribes of office, privilege (in the form of licences and exemptions) and cash. This phenomenon is commonplace in all state governments and hardly a rarity in the Delhi parliament. It is, of course, scandalous. The foreign correspondent is filled with righteous indignation at this abuse of democracy and even the man in the street rants against the politicians and their unprincipled methods. When the Congress boss in Orissa, having broken with his party, sneered 'Give me a crore* of rupees and I will become Prime Minister' it provoked an uproar. It was altogether too near the bone.

It thus comes as something of a surprise to learn that the administration in Gujerat is generally reckoned as one of the best in India. Or that Mrs. Gandhi has just pulled off the nationalisation of the banks. Contrary to every expectation things get done in India. It seems impossible that any request could ever penetrate the fences of red tape or scale the walls of corruption and double talk but suddenly it is there approved and actioned. Corruption is not necessarily detrimental to efficiency. Even where it has been replaced by red tape there is often a quick way round. Making a trunk call can be very frustrating so instead of 'ordinary' you make it 'urgent'. Hours elapse and nothing happens. You try offering the operator five rupees but he is not interested. The line is still busy. How, you wonder, can the country possibly operate if it takes so long to make a call? But look carefully in the phone directory and you'll discover the 'lightning' call. In minutes the line is cleared and you're through. You might even have tried 'priority' but for this you would need the sanction of a VIP.

Indian politicians hardly have a monopoly of double talk but there is something particularly offensive about the brazen floor-

* Instead of thousands and millions Indians count in *lakhs* and *crores*. The *lakh* is a hundred thousand and the *crore* ten million.

crossing however little it may affect the government's efficiency. It is surely misleading the electorate if you stand for election on one party manifesto and once elected promptly switch to another. To see your representative swallowing his fine words for the chance of a junior ministerial office or to see a five-party coalition doubling the number of ministerial sinecures to satisfy all groups is hardly edifying. The manipulation of democratic forms and procedures seems to matter more to most politicians than the business of legislation and government. But against this it is worth remembering that Indians as a whole have scant respect for ideologies. In Hinduism dogma is fluid and conflicting. In social life it's the appearance and behaviour of a man, be he Parsi or Jain, Christian or Brahmin which matters most, not his beliefs. So in politics whether your man belongs to one of the three socialist parties, two communist parties or two Congress parties scarcely matters. He is your man because through family, caste, community or professional affinity he is bound to your interests. Any means he can find to jockey into a position of power where he can advance these interests is worth considering. And the man in the street who startles you with revelations of corruption in high places is predictably someone whose candidate failed to get elected.

As the archetypal politicians the Congress-wallahs at Bombay airport are seldom as bad as they are made out to be. Unlike their Western counterparts they are easily approached; in the Delhi telephone directory the office and residence of every minister, M.P. and government official is listed. Even the Prime Minister holds a daily 'durbar', a sort of open house to which it is not difficult to gain access. In Parliament there may be a good deal of betel chewing and spitting, of ballot paper throwing and even physical violence—Indian arguments have a way of getting very heated. But all this is somehow preferable to the drab professionalism of Western politicians and the tireless exchange of innuendos and slights which so often passes for debate. At least Indian politics are exciting; they are rarely out of the headlines and command the sort of mass enthusiasm which in the West only football or scandal can expect.

Gandhi, who did more than anyone else to make the Indian people politically conscious, would probably have been embarrassed to see how politics-crazed the country has become. Disillusioned, many great men have turned away from the political scene. Gandhi himself seemed to be moving in the same direction before his assassination. Yet for all its abuses Indian democracy is alive. The credit must go to the men in *khaddi*, and their two father figures, Sivaji and Mahatmaji, the Mahratta warrior and the Gujerati saint. Militancy and non-violence, socialism and capitalism, idealism and venality, the paradoxes of the Indian politics pile up on one another. But to the Indian mind they are all just so many theories and theories are fun but they always conflict. What matters is the man and the moment. Sivaji making rings round the great Aurangzeb, Mahatmaji defying the British, Indiraji trouncing the Pakistanis. 'Bharata Devta', the Indian goddess, they were calling her after the 1971 war. That she had inspired victory was what mattered. The rights and wrongs of the situation were almost irrelevant.

# 6. GREAT OPEN SPACES

## Central India

North from Ahmedabad on the main line to Delhi the countryside starts one of those slow transformations so typical of the
subcontinent and so evocative of the slow progress of Indian
history. The lush greens of Gujerat begin to fade and the sleek
bossed cattle to give way to a smaller skinnier breed. Areas of
prickly scrubland intrude between the fields which in turn become
gradually stonier till they are indistinguishable from the surrounding desert. Of people or villages there is little sign, just miles of
rocky cactus country meeting the sky in a jagged range of distant
hills. The 'Thar', the great Indian desert, is beginning and the
train has slowed to a rolling chug for the climb on to its stark
upland. The long low howl of the whistle reverberates between
the hills; one thinks of the Union Pacific crossing hostile territory
in the West.

By the time you reach Abu Road the transformation is complete. So too is one's own acclimatisation. There seems nothing
extraordinary in the camels pulling carts, their shafts some twenty
feet long to reach the beast's shoulders, or in the hookahs which
vary from the elaborate hubble-bubble to a simple bowl and stem
like a briar pipe. Yet neither the camel nor the hookah is found in
the Deccan or the South. Both one associates more with the
Mohammedan world and with the desert. Here in the state of
Rajasthan, previously Rajputana, the aspect is distinctly Middle-
Eastern even if the tradition is strictly Hindu. One is back in a
world of sheep and goats, of robust meat-eating men, of tall,
often veiled women and of a semi-feudal chivalry. There is colour
in the scarlet of the Rajput turbans and the mirror-work blouses

of the peasant women but the cities are walled, the villages inward looking and the few roads hostile and deserted.

Dividing the North, the cradle of Hinduism and the core of Empire, from the South with its tropical profusion or the West with its commercial obsessions, lies a broad swathe of hills and plateau country. From the deserts of Rajasthan to the jungles of Madhya Pradesh and Orissa this difficult, sparsely populated and distinctly primitive belt forms the Great Divide of the sub-continent. To a large extent the invaders and conquerors, Aryan, Muslim and British, failed to penetrate it. Armies swept across the Malwa plateau and through the narrow corridor between the Aravalli and the Vindhya hills *en route* to contest the hegemony of the Deccan or ravage the shrines and seaports of Gujerat. They seldom turned aside to pursue the mirages as far as Jodhpur and Bikaner or to attack the elusive tribesmen east of Bhopal. The British *en route* to Delhi pushed their roads, railways and telegraph lines up from Bombay through the same corridor, but not until the present century was much done about radial lines in the same area.

Not surprisingly this vast wedge of India is today regarded as a primitive, feudal country in which lurk the dark forces of reaction. The Rajput princes and the aboriginal tribesmen are the delinquents in a modern socialist republic. The wealth and privilege of the one must be curbed, the education and social integration of the other promoted. Indian society is a long way from egalitarianism but whereas purely caste distinctions are proof against legislation those of feudal practice and tribal law are more vulnerable.

Rajputs claim to be descendants of the ancient Kshatriyas, the knights who were the second of the four 'varnas' in traditional Hindu law. This makes them a caste rather than a race but research now suggests that they are in fact descendants of invaders, Scythians or Huns, who followed the Aryan invasions. Having gained possession of the Doab (the area between the Ganges and the Jumna) they were driven from their prize to the desert and central highlands by another wave of invaders. Either way, whether a race or a caste—and once again the distinction in India is seldom

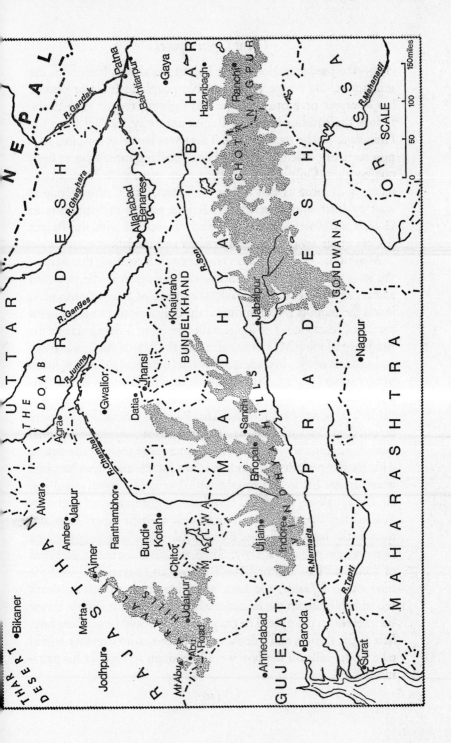

clear—the preoccupation of the Rajput has always been with the military calling of the Kshatriya. No people in India or outside has a longer or more distinguished fighting record than theirs. Before the Muslim invasions Rajput authority reached from the Himalayas to the Arabian Sea. There was never an empire; Rajputs were organised in clans and liked nothing more than to fight one another. Only rarely did they even manage to form a confederacy as loose as that of the Mahrattas. But if not by rule at least by birth and marriage the Rajput princes of Saurashtra in Gujerat are closely related and easily identified with the Rajput princes of far away Himachal Pradesh and Punjab.

Against the Muslim invaders in the twelfth century, throughout the long years of the Delhi Sultanate, and again in the sixteenth and seventeenth centuries against the spread of Moghul authority, it was the Rajputs who constituted the only serious and continuous thread of resistance. The juggernaut empire of Vijayanagar or the bands of galloping Mahrattas pall beside the Rajput's tireless bravery as defenders of Hindu tradition. Mewar (Udaipur), Marwar (Jodhpur), Amber (Jaipur), Bundi, Alwar, Kotah, Bikaner—every Rajput state has had its heroes and its hour of glory. The first was Prithviraj, king of the Chauhan Rajputs whose forces were defeated at Taraori in 1191. Delhi was lost, Ajmer his capital sacked, he himself was slain and his successors took to the desert. This set the pattern of Rajput warfare for the next five hundred years. Every battle was fought with incredible bravery and lost amidst appalling slaughter. Consistently outnumbered and outgunned the Rajput princes retired first to their desert forts and then to the barren hillsides. Every battle was a Thermopylæ or a Glencoe, every siege a Troy. Time and time again the garrisons of fortresses like Chitor, Ranthambhor and Merta followed the final rites of *Jauhar*, the men marching forth to certain death whilst behind them the flames crackled as their womenfolk threw themselves on the pyre. The only survivor would be a young boy, heir to the throne, and a defiant old princess, who together would take to the hills till the boy was old enough to recover his patrimony.

# Central India

Some of the greatest houses eventually came to terms with the Moghuls. Man Singh of Jaipur held high office in Akbar's army and thanks to this amnesty was able to start construction of the beautiful Amber Palace. The emperor married his daughter so that Jehangir was at least half Rajput. Udaipur on the other hand acknowledged Moghul sovereignty for only the briefest of periods. Even under Shah Jehan and Aurangzeb the famous line of heroic maharanas,* who claim descent from the Sun, was still defying every army sent against them. Until the present century it was their boast that never had they set foot in Delhi, the Moghul capital. But whether or not they joined the Moghuls the Rajput princes were recognised as self-governing by the British and allowed to retain their semi-independent status. To this treatment the princes responded and turned from the *Jauhar* to more peaceful tasks like polo, cricket and administration.

Their successors are the men who in the first full flush of independence rapture were talked and cajoled into merging their states in the new India. The motley collection of Muslim Nawabs and Nizams, and Mahratta Rajas, Maharajas and Gaikwars was dominated by the phalanx of Rajput princes. In Saurashtra alone there were some two hundred and twenty princely states most of them Rajput. Some had only a few acres of land but others thousands of square miles without which the map of India would be a sadly mottled affair. There were a few cases of intransigence and procrastination but by and large integration was achieved with amazing simplicity. Even today in their quarrel with the government few princes express any regrets over integration.

In return for the surrender of their sovereignty and independence the princes were allowed to retain most of the personal privileges of kingship—titles, palaces, sentries, tax exemption, freedom from import restrictions, etc.—and in addition were given an annual state subsidy called a privy purse, its size being related to the sort of income each house had previously enjoyed. In a socialist country this subsidising of a feudal aristocracy was obviously an

* Maharana is a Rajput title for Maharaja. The wife of either is a Maharani and their mother a Rajmata.

anomaly and few were the princes who expected that their privileges would go on indefinitely. They renounced their sovereignty and were duly praised for it. Why, I wondered, after private consultations could the same decorous and face-saving procedure not have been followed with regard to the privy purses and privileges?

We were on a long pier jutting out over a quagmire of mud which, just below where we sat, gave on to a lake. Together with the Maharani of B., her two daughters, son-in-law and the ADC we were having tea. Below us in the quagmire some thirty half-naked labourers and their womenfolk were endeavouring to create a terraced garden. I felt a little uncomfortable; it was too much like the Pharaohs taking their ease where they could watch the progress of a pyramid. But the others were quite oblivious that a building site should seem an odd place to be eating cucumber sandwiches and parading bone china. Her Highness, who stuck to betel nut from a silver cigarette box, had the old colonel, the ADC, dashing up and down with instructions about watering the roses and would they mind chanting a song or doing a tribal dance for us. He arrived back panting and slumped thankfully into a chair under one of the parasols.

The Maharani explained that she would be moving from the palace to this newer house as soon as the garden was ready. Shorn of her rank (though the telephone directory still listed her under H—'Her Highness, the Ex-ruler', etc.) it was better to live more modestly. One palace was already being run as a hotel by the son-in-law but the other two were too big and too old. Fortunately they could manage well enough without the subsidies and privileges, but what she objected to most was that the government and 'that woman' (Mrs. Gandhi) should deprive them of the people's respect as well as everything else. By making the abolition of the princely perquisites an election issue, by challenging the princes to fight for their rights and by thus making them scapegoats, the wretched politicians had made them forfeit the one thing they really did value, the affection and regard of their erstwhile subjects. To do without sentries was one thing but to

and still takes a paternal interest in its affairs. After independence he served as an Indian ambassador. If he is bitter he never shows it or if critical he never voices it. The discretion of a diplomat and the wisdom of age see him through crisis after crisis with a dignity that shames the aspiring hoteliers and the princely M.Ps.

Although many princes are Rajputs only a handful of Rajputs are princes. Most, although probably descended from or related to the Rajput warriors of old, are ordinary citizens claiming Rajput caste. The same, of course, applies to Brahmins of whom very few still pursue a priestly vocation. Were they still, I wondered, recognisable as Brahmins or Rajputs? Could one tell, say, a school-teacher of Brahmin caste from one of Rajput caste? Or indeed any other caste, subcaste or community where profession or dress did not give the game away? The nylon shirt and Gwalior suiting must make identification very difficult, but to the survival of caste in India this problem seemed crucial. If the only way of establishing a man's caste was by asking him, then clearly the whole structure could be undermined by simple misrepresentation. I asked G. He maintained that he could not only tell a Brahmin anywhere in India but that he could recognise one of his own sub-caste. He could also identify nearly all castes in his own locality though not outside it. How? Well it was a question of many things, name, behaviour, expressions, taste and so forth. He knew Englishmen who maintained that they could tell a public school boy from any other or a Wykehamist from an Etonian. It was the same thing only easier. If one was in doubt or wanted confirmation the simplest thing was to ask where a man came from.

Every visitor soon discovers that the eternal Indian question is 'where do you come from?' 'From which place do you come?' 'Where is your home?' 'What is your native place?' and so on through the gamut of extraordinary constructions taught as English in Indian schools. At first one regards this as showing a lively interest among Indians in the outside world. Sometimes this is the case but more often it is simply the traditional opening gambit. The name of a man's village, town or locality tells all. Invited to another's home his caste is immediately evident in the dress, the seclusion or otherwise of his wife, in their food, cooking, eating and so on. But failing such an invitation a clue as to the other's 'native place' is invaluable. All Rajputs do not live in Rajasthan, but on the other hand they don't just live wherever their fancy takes them. Every family has its ancestral town or village. And every village or town suburb is populated with only a handful of castes, perhaps one or two of Brahmin status and one of Rajput. The others will be professional castes easily identified by their trade. Even after several years as a teacher in Hazaribagh K. sees himself as stationed there. His home, he will tell you, is at Bakhtiyapur near Patna. And anyone who knows the caste distribution of Bihar will have him immediately classed as a Bhumihar Brahmin.

*   *   *

If caste identification is still possible amongst the professional classes of the new India it can be taken for granted amongst the lower classes. As so often privilege and status matter most to those who enjoy them least. In the case of the *Chamar* leather workers or the *Bhangi* sweepers a man's trade *is* his caste. Few societies have such a complicated lower stratum as the Indian. Besides the massive number of sub-castes of Sudra standing (lowest of the four Aryan *varnas*) there are two other groups customarily regarded as being outside society altogether. These are, on the one hand, the tribal peoples (or *Adivasis*\*) and, on the other, the Untouchables (also known as *pariahs*, outcastes or *Harijans*†). Though both are reckoned as beyond the pale of decent society only the tribals are outside the caste system. Untouchables not only belong to castes of their own but are just as discriminating amongst themselves as the touchable castes. The Indian Constitution recognises these two groups under the titles of 'Scheduled Tribes' and 'Scheduled Castes'. In Parliament and the State Assem-

---

\* *Adivasi* means aboriginal or pre-Aryan.

† Gandhi's euphemism for the untouchables. It means 'children of god' and is not much loved by those to whom it applies. There is too much suggestion of bastardy.

blies there are seats reserved solely for them and there are constituencies in which only they may stand. In addition there are
large job quotas in government service and place quotas in schools
which may only be filled by Scheduled Tribe or Caste members.
Society may discriminate against them but, in spite of its egali-
tarian principles, the Constitution discriminates for them.

There are said to be some forty million tribals (not 'tribesmen')
in India. They are scattered about the less accessible hills and
jungles from Burma and the Himalayas to the Nilgiris in the
South, but the greatest concentration is in Madhya Pradesh and
the neighbouring areas of Orissa, Bihar and Andhra. A jungle in
India is a bit like a forest in Scotland. It can be a tract of almost
treeless hillside or, like the western slopes of the ghats, the real
thing. In Madhya Pradesh the jungle is well wooded but not
impenetrable. The difficulties of getting around have more to do
with the rocky ravines, the crumbling hillsides and the vast distances. But three to four centuries ago when rhinoceros roamed
along the Ganges and most of north India was woodland these
central jungles were really inaccessible. Here the tribal people,
driven from the Gangetic plain by its succession of invaders, had
taken refuge. Some of the tribes are related to the Dravidians of
the South, others are the descendants of still earlier peoples of the
subcontinent, the true aboriginals whose only similarities are to
the world's oldest races, the African bushmen and the Australian
aboriginal. Such a people are the Mundas of Chota Nagpur, true
Australoids with splayed nostrils and low, broad foreheads.

Traditionally the tribals were semi-nomadic, some living exclusively off what they could hunt, others relying on the quick
cultivation of a few scratch fields. Nowadays most of them are
settled, but one may still come across the occasional Birhor, a
truly nomadic people who live solely off what the woods have
to offer. Near Ranchi (Bihar) one emerged cautiously on to the
roadside. He wore just a loincloth and carried a long pointed
stave. His hair was long and matted. Before the car reached him
he was gone, back into the woods like a shy animal. It was just a
glimpse but the stealth and speed of his movements told more of

his tribal history than any amount of interviewing would have been likely to elicit. Even in the settled tribes custom remains strong. In spite of Hindu influence many continue to bury their dead rather than burn them. Christian missionaries report that converted tribals after their church wedding usually return to their village for a marriage according to tribal custom.

Most tribal women have adopted the sari or its local equivalent but the colour is usually distinctive and they often dispense with the *choli* (bodice). In Chota Nagpur they go in for a white sari with a red or green border similar to those of Bengal but far narrower and usually of a quieter shade. By contrast I have never seen a gayer scene than that of tribal crowds waiting for a local train on Bhopal station. The porters in their crimson turbans and matching shirts usually catch the eye against the seething confusion of white cottons but here they were indistinguishable. It was largely because there were so many women about. Bright yellows, pinks, greens and scarlets, often all represented on the same person, made the place distinctly garish. I scanned the platform but could see no Murias. To many this is the best-known tribe because its women still wear no clothes above the waist. Calendars featuring Muria tribal scenes go down well in the more Westernised offices and seldom an election passes without the papers carrying photographs of polling in the Muria country.

Over the centuries the fringes of tribal territory have steadily receded. The sensitive, good-natured and gentle tribals were no match for the crusading incursions of Rajputs, Muslims and Mahrattas. They soon learnt the sad inadequacy of bow and arrow and examples of successful resistance are rare. On their western extremities in Maharashtra and Rajasthan the Bhil people still occasionally waylay travellers though they are now largely settled and Hinduised. They were too close to the main communications between North and South.

Farther east, Gondwana has a history of some note. The Gonds, the largest of the tribes, had a way of establishing their independence right up to the last century. From about A.D. 1200 there were as many as four independent Gond kingdoms. The Raja of one of the middle kingdoms founded Nagpur whilst his rival in the southern kingdom formed a corps of Janissaries called Tarvels whose initiation ceremony centred on the eating of wild orchids. The northern kingdom erupted into history under a Boadicean queen called Durgavati who killed herself after defeat by one of Akbar's generals. It is quite a jolt when Gond history actually touches that of India as a whole. Most of it reads like The Lord of the Rings; the Hobbit heroes would have made friends with these gentle Gonds and perhaps have joined the Tarvels on one of their campaigns against the Middle Kingdom. The Gond Rajas were possibly of mixed Rajput-Gond descent and a substantial class of Hindu Gonds arose through conversion and intermarriage. With the advent of the Mahrattas the true aboriginals withdrew farther into the jungles taking with them their beliefs in sylvan gods and the wicked spirits of cholera and smallpox.

There it fell to the missionaries to rediscover them. Whole tribes were converted to Christianity in marked contrast to the indifference shown by caste Hindus. Education was encouraged and even if traditional customs declined the tribes entered the twentieth century with a far better chance than their American or Australian counterparts. Their scheduled status in the Constitution is a real incentive, particularly the educational preferences and there is a law preventing an Adivasi from parting with his land to a non-Adivasi except with a magistrate's permission. Home-brewed beer and spirits play a large part in their lives. Coupled with a totally guileless nature this made them easy prey for less scrupulous profiteers and money-lenders. In addition to these safeguards tribals are now demanding a degree of political autonomy. There is a growing sense of community awareness as represented by parties like the Jharkhand of Chota Nagpur. Its electoral symbol is the tribal drum and its objective the formation of a tribal state in southern Bihar.

As with all Indian communities unity poses a problem and the Jharkhand is currently split into some four factions. The tribes even in this small corner of central India have little in common with one another. The predominantly Christian Oraons, the

Australoid Mundas, the primitive Birhors and the progressive Santhals with their beautiful women are all self-contained communities. Marriage or social contact between members of different tribes is as rare as between members of different castes. Most of the tribes like castes are divided into numerous sub-tribes and split into *gotras* (the lines of descent which determine who a caste member may or may not marry). Some tribes even have professional specialisations. There are whole Santhal villages which specialise in the manufacture of brass objects by the lost wax process and others who are traditionally iron smelters producing blades and arrow heads. Add to these a variety of agricultural specialities and one has a social set up very close to the caste system though without the religious sanction associated with the idea of caste *dharma*.

Tribal religion centres on the propitiation of spirits personified in the deities of smallpox, cholera and various local forest and fertility gods. Many of these have been incorporated into the Hindu pantheon as aspects of existing deities, especially Durga, or as separate ones. This does not make tribal religions Hindu; but it did make the acceptance of Hinduism a good deal easier for some of the tribal peoples. It is fashionable nowadays to conjecture how much in the way of religion and social organisation the tribes picked up from Hindu practice and how much early Hinduism might have borrowed from tribal practice. It seems likely for instance that a sort of caste system was practised by both Dravidians and Adivasis before the Aryans arrived.

However this may be, the gap in India between the aboriginal peoples and the majority community is nothing like as wide as between the American Indian and the white American or the Australian 'Abo' and the white Australian. The tribal communities, whilst retaining many of their traditional beliefs and some of their traditional way of life, are unquestionably participants in Indian independence. Yet if India has made a better job of integrating its primitive peoples and if, as is tempting, one ascribes this to some aspect of the Hindu genius for tolerance, the fact remains that the tribes are outcastes in Hindu society. It was not the Hindu way to convert, persecute or exterminate but the more subtle economic and social pressures were there. Sanskrit literature describes the noseless Dasyus, Dravidians and Adivasis, as outside the caste system. The higher classes of Dravidian society managed to scramble in over the centuries but few of the tribals gained acceptance. Those living in tribal areas were and still are largely unaffected by whatever status some remote society cares to accord them. But those who, centuries ago, did not take to the hills or the jungles were doomed to an even worse fate. Aryan conquest reduced them to a condition bordering on slavery and it is their descendants who, according to most authorities, are now the Untouchables, the butt for every kind of discrimination and the beast for every degrading activity.

The study of India's Untouchables is particularly fascinating because it exemplifies another set of very Indian contradictions. In the first place untouchability, even before the privileges of scheduled status, was not necessarily synonymous with poverty. Our rented house in Himachal had, like many other Indian houses, no lavatory. A sackcloth box was constructed round a hole in the garden to afford some privacy for the white man's sensibilities. As soon as possible the hole was to be superseded by a commode, the 'chaise percée' or 'thunderbox' of our grandparents. When after weeks it still had not appeared we were assured that there was no shortage of commodes; the town was full of them and the shortage was of sweepers. 'Sweeper' is a euphemism for someone who removes the contents of a commode from a commode or from any of the more public spots favoured by the local population. In this lies the degradation of his profession. But so scarce and reluctant are these functionaries in some areas that those pursuing the traditional calling may earn a considerable wage. Then there is the *dhobi* caste, washermen, whose willingness to handle other people's laundry brings a substantial income. At first it is difficult to see what is so degrading about washing clothes; the man in pyjamas who arrives on a bicycle to collect the laundry seems anything but downtrodden. But to the orthodox he is unclean and not to be welcomed into the house at any cost.

Soiled clothes are bad enough but is there not also the danger of contact with menstrual stains? The 'curse' in India is precisely that. It degrades womanhood and defiles whoever is actually suffering from it so that they too have a few days' taste of untouchability. The *dhobi* is permanently defiled by association with it.

Secondly, although the Untouchable's trade is originally responsible for his social degradation it does not follow that as soon as he takes to some other work he is rid of discrimination. Many reputable castes of agricultural labourers, construction workers and domestic servants were regarded as untouchable simply because caste sanctions still applied to them. The ultimate criterion was practice, whether the caste was allowed in or near a temple, well or school used by other castes and whether they were allowed the services of caste barbers and tailors. Even castes converted to Christianity might find that they were still untouchable. A church with two naves, one for the clean another for the unclean, was designed and elsewhere two communion services had invariably to be held. Castes regarded as untouchable in one area might be perfectly acceptable in another whilst degrees of discrimination could range from casual avoidance to attempts to impose restrictions of dress, housing, even income, on the unfortunates.

Under the Constitution of independent India untouchability is abolished. It is illegal to refuse to let a sweeper draw water, enter a temple and so on. This might be thought to have abolished the final criterion of untouchability but since the Constitution also seeks to help Untouchables and must therefore define them they emerge as 'Ex-Untouchables', 'Harijans' or 'Scheduled Caste Members'. Not only this but in order to get the jobs, scholarships and democratic privileges reserved for them they must declare themselves. 'Beware, he got a scholarship; he must be an Untouchable', or 'How can the secretariat increase efficiency when it must employ so many inexperienced staff simply because they have scheduled status?' are not uncommon sentiments.

By a curious coincidence the man who actually drafted the Constitution and so abolished untouchability was himself an

Untouchable. He was Dr. Ambedkar, Law Minister in Nehru's government and unquestioned leader of the underprivileged. Amongst the Untouchables he enjoys semi-divine status and no Harijan home is complete without his photograph. His great enemy was Mahatma Gandhi, the one other man who was interested in arousing the national conscience over the plight of the Untouchables. Their quarrel is one which still divides the ranks of their lowly followers. Gandhi had nothing against the caste system. 'If Untouchability and caste are convertible the sooner caste perishes the better. But I am satisfied that caste is a healthy institution.' Ambedkar disagreed. Not only must caste go if Untouchability was to be eradicated but the whole of Hinduism must fall if caste went. Buddhism, the ancient reformed religion of India, was the answer. Many Untouchables, though devoted to Baba Sahib Ambedkar, would not go so far. Like Gandhi they respected caste and their highest ambition was to climb on to its lowest, touchable rung. Sudra status would do fine for Untouchability, not caste, was the *bête noire*. But a few, particularly among his fellow Mahars in Maharashtra, followed Ambedkar into a self-proclaimed neo-Buddhism. Most of Buddha's high ideals were lost on them; Ambedkar is their real god and Hinduism still their way of life and form of ritual. But Buddhism excludes caste and therefore Buddhist they are.

This had interesting repercussions in the political sphere since a self-proclaimed Buddhist, though everyone knows he must be an Untouchable (the only other Indian Buddhists are, like the Ladakhis, largely Mongol, Himalayan people), cannot qualify as a member of a scheduled caste. To be of a caste he must be a Hindu. Therefore he misses out on the jobs and scholarships. The Untouchables, like every other community in India, have their political party. In this case it is the Republican Party of India founded by Dr. Ambedkar. One of its main objectives is to secure recognition as a scheduled caste for the Buddhists of India.

If there is irony here one has only to look further at the party's manifesto to better it. It sounds almost contradictory to read that another of the party's objectives is the abolition of the scheduled caste's job quota in the administrative services. This is sought because the community's radicals feel that too many of its educated potential leaders are being wooed away from the true cause, alleviating the lot of Untouchables, by the security and pay of an establishment job. The quota system is seen as a deep Congress plot to sap the masses of their natural leaders, to place them under an obligation to the government and the higher castes and so to win votes.

The allegation is worth note because in the case of the Untouchables government patronage is condoned and therefore visible. India has had the same ruling party since before Independence—nearly thirty years. There must come a time when one has a right to ask whether a change of government is practically possible. And if not whether democracy can really be said to be working. The fortunes of the Congress Party have waxed and waned and waxed again but even in its darkest moments it still had a crushing majority over any of the opposition parties. Their attempts to form alliances, united fronts and so on are a measure of their exasperation in trying to match the Congress monolith. Aside from the instances of bribery and corruption noted earlier the colossal administration is now regarded not as an impartial executive but as fair game in the field of party politics. It is assumed that under Congress rule jobs go to Congress voters. Given a thirty-year span this leaves little room for any but Congressmen in the service. And once the whole administration is seen as a source of patronage the prospect of a government falling looks remote indeed. In no sense is Congress particularly to blame; other parties while enjoying power in the states have shown themselves, if anything, more willing to try their hand at patronage. At the same time this grudge of the Untouchables and the Republican Party is common to most other parties. The Akalis would say that good Sikhs were wooed into the Congress ranks and the D.M.K. that good Tamil separatists were lost in this way.

Another avenue for the advancement of Untouchables—and one fraught with less difficulties—is the provision of alternative employment in an independent setting. South from Madras on

served memory of their British connections and the preferences enjoyed while British rule lasted leads them to expect rather more in the way of job opportunities and social recognition than is the outcaste's lot. V. S. Naipaul paints a pathetic picture\* of elderly Anglo–Indians in Madras talking of home as an England they have never seen and reverencing a faded photo of some long-dead gunner as if it were a holy picture. Even their parliamentary leader, Mr. Frank Anthony, admits that he represents a community too proud and too desperate to acknowledge itself. Numerically small, socially disparate and geographically scattered it is if anything surprising that they are still recognisable as a community.

Probably this is due to a certain professional cohesion. Anglo–Indians are particularly identified with British institutions and still continue in the face of stiff competition to seek employment in the army or post and telegraph services. Or, above all, the railways. There are a few exclusively Anglo–Indian settlements with improbable names like McLuskieganj near Ranchi but chiefly they live in towns and especially those like Jhansi or Jabalpur with large railway junctions or workshops. A good command of English and a taste for clerical work produced something close to a caste of booking clerks and ticket collectors. One is reminded of the Goanese cooks and singers but whereas they have established their trade status the Anglo–Indians have virtually lost theirs.

Indian Railways is nowadays a unique and supremely Indian institution. Companies like the Grand Indian Peninsular Railway, the first to link Delhi and Bombay, made India workable as a national entity. The legacy was, of course, British but the enjoyment of it is a totally Indian experience. Although the whole colossal network is divided into regional groupings it is essentially a pan-Indian institution. But whereas the Ganges steamers or the coastal shipping had provided local communications in the north and south the railways made their greatest contribution in spanning the vast open spaces of central India. No visitor should leave India without embarking on one of those long journeys through

\* In *Area of Darkness.*

Rajasthan or Madhya Pradesh. For an insight into the Indian way of life, for a taste of its beauty, its excitements and its frustrations, the experience can hardly be bettered.

The fun starts when you go to buy a ticket. There is, of course, no problem. Anyone can buy a journey ticket from the booking office right up to the moment the train leaves. But without a reservation a journey ticket is useless; Indian trains are invariably full, tickets are issued for a specific train only and the procedure for obtaining a refund is so daunting as to be unthinkable. So you move to the queue for a reservation ticket, only to discover that before you can get this you need a form. Nothing ever happens without a form and the forms come not from the reservations office or the booking office but the inquiry office. You are standing in your third long queue before you have even started. The form requires a good deal of thought; age and sex are demanded along with the number of your train, several signatures and 'any special requests'. The Indian passion for categorisation means that there are about six classes of travel from which to choose before you can even start to think of special requests. Back to the reservations queue where eventually the harassed clerk scrutinises the form for omissions and with what sounds like a sigh of disappointment turns to a pile of enormous dog-eared ledgers. Your train, inevitably, is fully booked. You can be twenty-second on the waiting list or travel two days later. The agonising decision has to be made immediately unless you are prepared to face the queue yet again. You opt to travel two days later. He scribbles on the back of the form and returns it.

'What about the reservation ticket then?'

'First you must take one journey ticket. You are getting that from the booking office. Then I am issuing one reservation ticket.'

Back to the booking office queue, back again to the reservations office queue and you're almost there. The man in front of you has a South Indian name of thirty-one syllables. Painfully the clerk copies them out and the seconds tick past. Twelve-thirty and with a crash the shutters fall. Lunch hour. Or perhaps you just make it. But it's one rupee for the reservation ticket, you have only a ten-rupee note and as usual no one has any change. It's off to the bookshop or the restaurant to make a swop and back again to the end of the queue.

After a while one learns of the many short cuts. The waiting list is never as hopeless as it sounds. Even twenty-second place is more often accommodated than not. Every train and plane in India has an enormous quota of seats withheld until the last minute in case a party of V.I.P.s wishes to travel. One can even qualify for this quota if one takes the trouble of visiting the railway head-quarters and impressing on them the urgency of one's journey. Alternatively you can just turn up at the station and without journey ticket or reservation ticket march confidently on to the train. It's amazing how often accommodation can be found by a helpful conductor.

Just as surprising in view of all the red tape, the piles of ledgers and stacks of forms, is that when days later you present yourself at what may even be a different station there on the carriage door is your name. In some extraordinary way the whole system works. You settle in and give an order for lunch, tea, dinner, morning tea and breakfast the following day and with uncanny precision each in due course arrives exactly as ordered. Like Indian Airlines the whole system seems appallingly inefficient but unlike the airlines the railways are reliable. Trains are not fast but they are rarely more than a few minutes late. Monkeys change the signals, left-wing students derail the engines, floods wash away the track, passengers lean on the communications cord and cows fall asleep on the line yet somehow the trains keep running. It's all so very typical of India. It can't work but it does.

Even if the system has its failings one is prepared to forgive Indian railways a good deal. The romance of travelling on the Frontier Mail, the Malabar Express, the Black Diamond Express or the Kashmir Mail and of hearing the steam engines chugging through the night is matched only by the insight afforded by the railways into the Indian way of life. Every station is a microcosm of its town or village. Whole families seem to cook, eat, sleep and occasionally work there. On the platforms children are born and suckled, people grow old and die—all within full view of the 15 Up, the 22 Down, the 15 Down and the 22 Up. In the first-class waiting-room businessmen hold conferences, in the restaurant they entertain their clients and in the retiring rooms over a bottle of Black Knight whisky they dictate their correspondence. In every third-class carriage there develops a tight little social world where in intense discomfort the carefully defined network of human relations may be observed amidst the shouting, the laughter and the untuned blaring of a transistor. From Kipling's day to Kushwant Singh's* whole villages rise, eat and sleep to the rhythm of the 'te-rains' comings and goings. Castes of plate layers and tea sellers have grown up round the system. Through the deep sleep of the first-class passengers comes the sound of the latter's croaking chants.

> Chai, char, garum char.
> Chai pio, char pio, garum char.

It sounds like a mantra every bit as holy as Hare Krishna.

Some recollections are so vivid that they come to eclipse all others. Out of tens of thousands of miles covered in the reassuring familiarity of Indian Railways one journey stands out. It was from Gwalior to Sanchi south through the Bundelkhand area of Madhya Pradesh. The train was, I think, the Punjab Mail nearing the end of the first of its two days' journey to Bombay. Our compartment had a door opening not on to the corridor but on to the great outside. I sat on the floor with legs dangling, no doubt illegally, outside the train. The sun had lost its heat and the light was that special golden refulgence which bathes the dullest countryside in startling beauty. The telegraph wires were dotted like a music score with random notes in the shape of the black, long-tailed drongos. Beyond and below stretched fields of wheat and stockades of sugar cane, relieved by the occasional pool with just the heads of a herd of buffalo like so many crocodiles breaking the still surface. The train was not scheduled to stop at the little

* See *Last Train to Pakistan*.

station of Sanchi but a word with the conductor had apparently fixed everything; besides this journey could go on indefinitely as far as I was concerned.

We passed Datia and Jhansi where the distant hills draw nearer and each one seemed to be crowned with some crumbling fort. There was a ridge so spiky with the *sikharas* of a long cluster of white temples that it looked like a dinosaur. Then through a densely wooded belt, the home of tigers and tribals, and back on to a long stretch of farming country. A herdsman was driving home his cattle, four white cows against the golden green of a paddy field. The dust rose beneath their feet and hung in the air like smoke. The world was still; it was all so peaceful. When the train slowed for a signal I was tempted to jump. It was the excitement of having made what seemed then a real discovery. There were no fences. To most this is probably a fairly obvious feature of the Indian countryside. But somehow I had missed it and the sudden realisation produced something like a brainstorm. No fences, no dry stone walls or prickly hedges, no slicing highways or striding pylons, the freedom to roam at will in a land where there is no regimentation and where each man knows his place. I could feel strongly the urge which might take a respectable family man away from his home and job to become a wandering Sannyasi.* Or the attraction of the picaresque for the itinerant musicians, snake charmers and saddhus. To wander across this vast open land, over the warm brown soil, along these endless paths leading God knows where, to be at home in every village, to admire the cattle, sample the crops and to sit in the dust and talk with the farmers—above all to go on and on without knowing restriction or rejection, this seemed the great attraction. Just as fences are unnecessary since everyone knows what land is his to cultivate or graze so in society everyone knows and respects his status and that of others. Strife is certainly not eliminated but the insecurity which makes one man an exhibitionist, another a hypocrite, a third a snob, is rare. Psychological barriers are as

---

* A renunciate. Usually someone who has acquired something worth renouncing—family, position or wealth—and is no longer in his youth.

scarce as fences and traditional Indian society one of the most accommodating in the world.

★   ★   ★

Along with the renunciates, the saddhus, the pilgrims, the party workers and the snake charmers there is now an influential body of social workers wandering over the face of the countryside. These are not eager young people trying to help the aged or educate the children but highly respected celebrities fired with a revolutionary zeal to cure the country's ills at source. Their leader is Vinobha Bhave of the *Bhoodan* movement who for decades has been tramping through the villages in the best Gandhian fashion persuading landowners to give up their land for redistribution among the landless. He offers nothing in return except perhaps a poorly printed paperback of the Gita. But then he is a saint. It must be quite difficult for a god-fearing laird to slam the door in his face. In every state there is now a land ceiling. No one is allowed to own more than thirty or so acres. Yet by parcelling the estate out amongst relatives, fictitious or otherwise, and bribing the administration, the landlords linger on. The endeavours of Bhave are faithfully reported by the newspapers and in some areas have had sensational results.

His most distinguished disciple is Jayaprakash Narayan—'J.P.' to the Indian public—a close associate of Nehru's and at one time regarded as his successor. But he grew disillusioned with politics and wandered off to join Bhave. His political utterances still make the headlines and there is no man in India whose opinions are so widely respected. The year 1972 saw him in the Chambal Valley a few miles west of where we were rolling south in the Punjab Mail. Besides its tribals and princes the central divide of India is renowned for its criminal castes, especially robbers, 'dacoits', and nowhere more so than the ravines of the Chambal Valley. 'J.P.' was there not to encourage the police or assist the harassed locals but to deal direct with the bandits. Like Bhave he had nothing to offer, not even an amnesty. He was relying entirely on his own reputation and a chance of convincing them that their way of life was not just illegal but also contrary to Hindu scripture.

A few weeks later the papers were full of it. This is the *Sunday Statesman*.

JAURA APRIL 14.—About a hundred of the dreaded Chambal Valley dacoits laid down their arms here today before an image of Mahatma Gandhi and a badly drawn sketch of Acharya Vinobha Bhave and the 30,000 who came to see the spectacular 'change-of-hearts' ceremony wondered if peace had really descended on the troubled terrain.

On the simply decorated dais were the Sarvodaya leader, Jayaprakash Narayan, and the Chief Minister of Madhya Pradesh, Mr. C. P. Sethi, who hugged and patted the desperadoes as they trooped past, bowing repeatedly.

The scenario on the stage was simple: a dacoit climbs the stairs from the right, places his gun and ammunition before the image and the sketch, touches Mrs. Narayan's feet, shuffles towards Mr. Narayan who rises and hugs him, touches Mr. Sethi's feet who without rising pats him, a priest hands him a copy of the Gita and the Ramayana (the illiterate are expected to learn to read and write in jail—their reformatory) while a dozen *khaddi*-clad Gandhians shout: 'Gandhiji ki jai'.★

The new convert waves to the crowd who cheer in direct proportion to the awe in which they hold the bandits on the stage.

For instance the loudest cheer went up for Mohar Singh, the dark, heavily built king of the Chambal wanted for nearly 100 murders and numerous cases of plunder, sporting a ferocious moustache curling up to his temple. In fact Mohar Singh, who had even threatened to murder Mr. Sethi, submitted a note to the Chief Minister urging him to persuade his (Mohar Singh's) enemies to surrender their arms as well so that no harm comes to his family and friends.

And so on.

★ 'Victory to Gandhi' or just 'Hail Gandhi'.

# Great Open Spaces

Not so many miles to the east of Jhansi, J.P.'s next target for dacoit conversion, lies the remote temple complex of Khajuraho. Dating from the tenth century it is unique in northern India where Hindu shrines were largely destroyed by the Muslim invaders. This, however, is not why every tour of India includes a trip to this isolated site or why there is a new airport with daily flights from Delhi and a mushrooming collection of tourist bungalows and hotels. Mention the primitive character of Madhya Pradesh and few will assume you are referring to dacoits or tribals or princes. Surely you must mean the erotic sculptures and friezes of Khajuraho. The bookshops in Delhi are full of coffee table works in full colour on the wonders of Khajuraho, the tourist brochures speak of the place as if it were the greatest shrine in India and the visitors come away raving about the architecture. One is reminded of the publishers who recommend that you read the *Kamasutra* because it is a literary classic. The sculptures of Khajuraho, or those of Konarak in Orissa, are undoubtedly beautiful but it is by virtue of their subject matter that they have attracted attention and it is for this that the tired tourist slung with cameras waits vacantly in the early morning at Delhi airport.

The erotic sculptures, like the *Kamasutra*, are explicit. They portray couples in the many variations of the act of love and do so with a gentle dignity unknown to our sex-crazed society. Whole books have been written about the Hindu obsession with eroticism and love-making. What are entwined couples doing in a temple or the *Kamasutra* amongst the predominantly religious treatises of Hindu literature? What, for that matter, is the role of sexuality in a society which to Western minds is puritanical in the extreme? My wife and I were almost lynched when on Pathankot station we flew into each other's arms after a long separation. Even American comedy films have to be expurgated before they go on release. Did the whole sexual theme develop from the fertility symbols of *lingam* and *yoni* (phallus and vagina) which are to be found in most temples or has it something to do with the aberrations of Tantricism? Or is it just an example of the Indian zest for life in all its forms?

In both literature and sculpture there is an overriding tendency to analyse, enumerate and categorise*. One sees it in the listing of the seven forms of yoga, the sixty-four rishis, the four states of consciousness and so on. The seven types of kiss listed in the *Kamasutra* or the eight types of love bite place this work firmly in the same tradition. The three attitudes of the Buddha, the nine avatars of Vishnu, the fifty-two jinas take the same tradition into sculpture. On the trains every fan and fitting in the compartment has a boldly stencilled reference number and nothing can compare with an Indian business letter for references—'Yours of 13th ref. TB/104/AX/7569Supt/41', etc. The caste system with its four *varnas* and numerous but always explicit and listed subdivisions is another example. Everything it seems must fit into some dimly perceived cosmic order of things which out of the complex mathematics of the world of gods and men is finally reducible to the beautiful simplicity of the All, Brahman, the Godhead, the One.

Religion embraces everything. Warriors must fight because it is their *dharma* and die not in slavery but in a *Jauhar*, dacoits surrender not to the law but to the Gita and politicians bow to the saints. For the Brahmin at least, how and when to make love is carefully laid down by caste customs and religious sanction. Love-making, like everything else, has its place in the great scheme of things. Its pleasurable as well as its procreational aspect must be accommodated. Unlike Christianity Hinduism appreciates this and finds even in the temple a place for eroticism. It is sad that even some Indians find this embarrassing and dismiss it as primitive.

* Not surprisingly the Indian contribution to mathematics was considerable. It includes the numerical system (called Arabic because Europe learnt it from the Arabs), logarithms and the concept of zero.

# 7. THE SOPHISTICATED AND THE SIMPLE

## Eastern India

Before the partition of the subcontinent into India and Pakistan eastern India was a well-defined area. It consisted of Bengal, Assam and the surrounding hill areas, a region dominated by its rivers and by the great city of Calcutta. The Ganges and the Brahmaputra, after flowing for hundreds of miles straight towards each other, turn south and splay out. In thousands of channels ranging from broad turgid waterways to narrow irrigation streams they wander and ooze across the waterlogged countryside fanning out into the Bay of Bengal. From the air there is no coastline. The islands, mudbanks and tongues of mainland look like debris washed down into the sea; miles out from land the sea is still a rich brown. The role of these rivers as great Indian sewers was neatly complemented by that of Calcutta in the human geography of the area. Situated on the Hooghly river, the most western of these channels, it was the clearing port for the produce of the whole region. Jute from East Bengal, coal from West Bengal and Bihar and tea from Assam all passed through Calcutta. With them came the population of Bengalis, Biharis and a few Assamese who have made the city the world's fourth largest.

Since 1947 East Bengal (now Bangladesh) with its largely Muslim population has been severed from the rest of the region. For the traveller this means that to get by rail from Calcutta to Assam entails two days of rattling over endless bridges all the way to the Nepalese border, shunting back and forth through the narrow corridor between East Bengal, Nepal and Sikkim and then doubling back down to the Brahmaputra valley. Calcutta lost most of its jute trade and West Bengal, the Indian half of the province, its market for coal in the East. In every sense except that of religion the partition of Bengal was a tragedy.

But as if this were not enough, eastern India has acquired a reputation for every kind of natural and human disaster. Typhoons and tidal waves sweep up from the Bay of Bengal, floods sweep down and after each crisis famine threatens. Over-population, intense poverty, communal violence and left-wing agitation are common on both sides of the political frontier. When in 1971 the East finally opted for statehood independent of Pakistan it was inevitably the tragedies which made the news—massacres, atrocities, refugees and, once again, famine.

To this catalogue of horrors Calcutta makes its own special contribution. Its very name is horrifying, a derivation from Kali,★ the blood-curdling aspect of Durga who wears a necklace of skulls and drools over human sacrifices. Early French travellers mis-named it Golgotha, the field of skulls, and association with the macabre continued when some British troops suffocated in the Black Hole. Today Calcutta is synonymous with urban chaos, appalling housing, colossal unemployment, disastrous labour relations, rebellious students and political instability.

There is always a good enough reason for not going there. The city is 'bandh', on general strike, cholera has broken out, the monsoon is beginning or students are rampaging through the streets. Eventually you steel yourself to make the journey but flights are fully booked for weeks ahead. You are dissuaded from the luxurious Rajdhani Express because with its higher fare struc-ture it has become the prime target for left wing saboteurs; instead you settle for the modest Sealdah Express. Crossing from Bihar into West Bengal the air grows hotter and the sky becomes cloudy with smoke. Pithead wheels, slag heaps and belching chimneys slip past, interspersed with rank, dust-coated vegetation and pools of black slime. I imagined this lasting till the outskirts of Calcutta but suddenly the sky cleared and we were swaying through a smiling land of paddy fields and coco-nut palms. It was

★ Originally it was Kali-ghat, Kali's bank (on the river Hooghly).

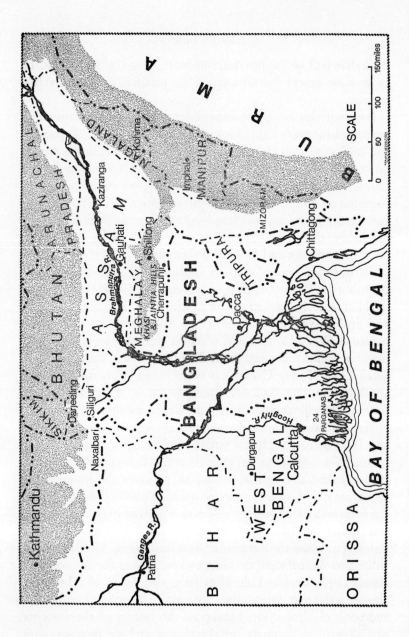

rather like Kerala with abundant irrigation channels, palm thatched huts and toddy shops.

The train began to fill as station followed station with growing rapidity. Suburban trains hurtled past, a blur of brown arms and legs projecting from their open doors and windows. People were dressed chiefly in white. A bright red border on the women's saris and a splash of scarlet on the forehead and in the partings of the hair was the only colour. To a Hindu the head is the most important part of the body. The slightest drop in temperature necessitates a scarf or shawl to protect it from cold. Oil and *ghi* are rubbed into the hair by both sexes, widows must cover their heads with the end of the sari (a point Mrs. Gandhi seldom neglects) and even the poorest street-dwellers devote hours to delousing one another's scalps. The red forehead *tilaka* is worn by every respectable married woman but it is only in northern India that they go in for the red partings.

After miles of flats and factories I was ready for the nightmare which must surely begin at Sealdah station, one of the city's two termini. And it did. There were no taxis—on strike—so we set off by rickshaw. In Delhi a rickshaw is a modified motor-cycle or scooter, in Lucknow or Benares it is a modified bicycle but in Calcutta it's just a man with a cart. Harnessed between the shafts he launches into a perilous trot through the crowded streets. As we passed through Chinatown with its Chinese butchers and shoemakers I vaguely recalled scenes of mandarins tossing firecrackers at the rickshaw puller's feet to urge him on. But here it would have been a waste of time. The congestion of people, carts, lorries, cars, cows and beggars was too dense. Inured as one becomes to poverty and squalor, I was still stunned by the chaos and desperation. The plight of the poor is often dignified, almost beautiful, but in Calcutta it is neither. Always it is tragic but the loss of dignity, the debasement of the human spirit, was somehow new and infinitely more horrifying. In Delhi it is surreptitiously that an old woman delves into the rubbish but here whole families were crawling about in piles of refuse seemingly left out for them on purpose. In broad daylight and without shame children fought over a coco-nut husk or snatched from their mother a rotting banana. Back in the villages when the food runs out the people wait. A deputation sets off to the nearest town to seek help. Those remaining kill the poultry and start praying. In Calcutta it seemed that such patience and resignation had been forgotten. The city has taught people a different way of life. Survival, like success, is something to be fought for. The enemy is not fate or some evil spirit but your neighbour.

Resentment, bitterness and intolerance, attitudes seldom found in rural India, seemed to be the order of the day. In Trivandrum, the capital of Kerala, it is said that half the bus drivers are B.A.s, some even M.A.s. I have no idea what the figures for educated unemployed in Calcutta may be nor how many qualified graduates have to settle for more menial jobs. But they must be considerable because with this class, rather than with the unemployed labourers, most of the urban trouble starts. West Bengal and Calcutta in particular has a vast middle class. Their first taste of competition comes with the examination system. To get any sort of job you need to be qualified. Qualifications mean status and income and these to the urban middle class are as important in India as anywhere.

'Excuse me, sir, you are not minding me asking you these questions?' We were on the bus to Puri. It was hot and noisy. Half the passengers had fallen asleep in their seats, an enviable achievement in which all Indians are adept. I only wished my neighbour would follow their example even if it meant having his prickly head lolling on my shoulder. I had already gathered that he was a grade three clerk, earned five hundred rupees a month and was very happy to meet an Englishman.

'I'm sorry, what were you saying?'

'I am asking, sir, what job will you give me in England? I am clerk grade three and earn five hundred rupees a month.'

'Well, I don't actually employ anyone but you shouldn't have much difficulty finding an office job in England.'

'Sir, I am asking you. You must give me a job.'

'But I don't need anyone.'

'You mean that you refuse to give me a job? Why you say this? I am forty-three. I speak English well, no?'

'Very well but it's nothing personal. I just couldn't afford to pay you.'

'Sir, I am asking this as a friend and you refuse me? I can be of service to you. How much will I earn?'

'Maybe two thousand rupees a month but not from me.'

'Sir, may I please be knowing your profession?'

'I am writing a book.'

'What sort of books are you writing?'

'Travel.'

'*Nowel?*'

'No, travel.'

'Not a *nowel?*'

'No, *trawel.*'

'Ah, *trawel.* Then you are not a specialist?'

'No, I suppose not.'

'Sir, I am a specialist, clerk grade three. Perhaps you are having one friend with profession who will give me a job.'

To an Indian the idea of someone who just mucks along, changing his job frequently, dabbling in many professions or playing the dilettante is totally incomprehensible. With the possible exception of Russia no society in the world is so imbued with graded professionalism. Amongst the trading castes this is hardly surprising but it applies just as rigorously to teachers, civil servants and businessmen. The concept of *dharma* attaches to every career and makes the acquisition of qualifications doubly significant. No one can afford to fail an examination because this means not just a lower income but also a certain falling short in the pursuit of one's *dharma*. A middle-class parent will be as busy as the child fixing things so that nothing stands in the way of his achieving a medical degree or an engineering qualification. For the child to enjoy the professional *dharma* into which he has been born it is essential.

Calcutta University has about two hundred thousand students.

## The Sophisticated and the Simple

Teaching here as in most Indian schools and colleges goes on in shifts from dawn to dusk. Secondary and higher education has become a machine churning out millions of qualified graduates and certificate holders a year. In most colleges well over ninety per cent of the pupils habitually sail through their exams. Cheating is so normal it is rarely even criticised. Prior release of the examination questions and bribing of the staff to elicit a satisfactory answer to them is common but still there seem to be students who cannot achieve the low standards required. The parents bribe and cajole, the students threaten and terrorise and eventually the poor examiners capitulate. Any attempt to get tough by reducing the number of passes to seventy per cent brings the students out on the streets and the whole community is held to ransom.

The effect of this farcical system on, for instance, recruitment to the medical profession is too frightening to contemplate. But in other spheres it is almost as disastrous. Qualifications remain an essential for any worth-while job but they are doled out so freely that most of the B.A.s and B.Sc.s find that they cannot get the jobs for which they consider they are qualified. Thousands take to the streets in their bitterness and begin to question the whole basis of their society and traditional beliefs. Calcutta with its large educated middle class, its menacing recession and its terrible poverty is especially vulnerable. The result is a revolutionary atmosphere which requires only a spark of militancy and a touch of ideology to explode in the best Marxist style. Or rather it would if this were not India. In fact all the ingredients are there but nothing has as yet happened.

For the British of Kipling's day the Bengali *babu* was an exasperating but seldom dangerous figure. Plump and jolly he was happiest crouched behind a desk amidst an intricate web of red tape or churning out a torrent of lively copy in atrocious English for the local press. Spouting Shakespeare over his mushy dinner of fish and rice he was a dead loss so far as the army was concerned. It came as a pleasant surprise for the Sahibs to discover that further west there were stalwart meat- and wheat-eating men like the

Rajputs and the Sikhs who would happily defy anyone for the regimental colours. The Bengali could be left to explore the delights of common law and assist in the administration.

And so he did until the independence struggle called forth heroic qualities of which no one could have suspected him. Passionate orators and heavily committed columnists were to be expected of Bengal but not a great and single-minded leader like Subhas Chandra Bose ('Netaji'). When one thinks of Indian leaders, the ascetic Mahatma and the cerebral Pandit spring to mind. In his way Bose was just as remarkable and, as a father figure of modern India, is as widely revered. By the empire he did the unforgivable when in 1941 he escaped from imprisonment in India to seek aid and propaganda facilities from Nazi Germany. Two years later he reappeared under Japanese auspices as Supreme Commander of the Indian National Army (the I.N.A.) and Head of State in the Provisional Government of Azad Hind (Free India). Along with the Japanese his forces, recruited largely from Indian prisoners of war, were poised for invasion on the borders of Bengal and Assam whilst in the Andaman Islands he already had a piece of Indian territory nominally under the authority of his government. The little Bengali in jack boots—his personal style owed not a little to *Il Duce* and the *Führer*—was on the brink of realising his wildest ambition. Like so many Indian leaders he had been deeply attracted by the life of the mystic but this, along with a brilliant career in the Indian Civil Service,* he had rejected in favour of a total commitment which appalled even the leaders of the Congress Party.

Two years later his whole world had collapsed. With his army discredited, and his government looking ridiculous he struggled back through Burma and South-East Asia. News of the Japanese surrender reached him near Singapore. His response seems to have been anything but despair. He had backed the wrong horse; now he would try the Russians. A seat was found on a Japanese flight to Manchuria. Bose took it and was never seen again. Probably it

---

* Gandhi, Nehru and Patel were all lawyers. Of all the independence leaders only Bose was that most exalted of beings, an I.C.S. man.

crashed in Formosa with Bose escaping and dying in hospital.*
That, at least, was the story of his companion though many
Indians today do not accept it. Attempts to set up inquiries into the
incident are a common feature of radical manifestos; like the
Mahdi his reappearance is daily expected. In beret and thick
round spectacles his flat Bengali face peers out of endless photographs; underneath are the words 'Jai Hind' (Victory to India),
the slogan which is his peculiar legacy to India and which is
shouted at every political rally regardless of party and appended to
every official statement however non-violent its sentiments.
Though the Forward Bloc, a radical Socialist party formed by
Bose before he escaped to Germany, still plays an important role
in Bengali politics, his political heirs are scattered more widely.
For the extreme right-wing parties like the Jan Sangh as well as
for the Communist left the dedication of Bose and the legend
of his life is sufficient justification for ignoring the pacifism
of Gandhi. And for the young educated Bengali, baulked of
the desk, the column or the bench which should have been
his by right, 'Netaji' is an example of militancy much to his
taste.

Into this revolutionary situation the final ingredient, Communist ideology, has been received with open arms. Though it
was Kerala that first elected a Communist dominated state government, far more significance is attached to the Communist hold on
West Bengal and to the two short-lived United Front Governments in which they have participated. West Bengal is nearly
part of South-East Asia. Its northern extremities extend to the
Chinese border and its role in the industrial and cultural life of
India is crucial. The Malabar coast is such a confusion and Kerala
such a political maverick that few would read any national
significance into its voting patterns. But West Bengal is very
different. A strong Communist government here would be cause
for international concern.

Just as India has two Congress parties and two Socialist parties,

* This interpretation and account of Bose's last days are taken from C. H. M. Toye's
biography of the I.N.A. leader *The Springing Tiger: story of a Revolutionary*.

so there are at least two Communist parties. The Communist Party of India (C.P.I.) is strongly pro-Moscow and is currently allied with Mrs. Gandhi's ruling Congress. Considerably more formidable is the Communist Party (Marxist) (C.P.M.), a doctrinaire organisation committed to solving India's problems by overthrowing the Constitution from within. Further left still are the Naxalites with a small pro-Mao party organisation known as the Communist Party (Marxist–Leninist) (C.P.M.–L.). This is not a political party in the democratic sense since they scorn the idea of standing for election, albeit as a means of overthrowing the Constitution. Just as Bose reached the conclusion that Independence was something that had to be taken by force and, if necessary, from outside so the Naxalites seek to destroy the existing order by borrowing from the example of the Vietcong and the Pathet Lao. Agrarian revolt, industrial anarchy and selected assassinations are their weapons.

No government in West Bengal has yet lasted its full five-year term. Election fever is a more or less permanent state of affairs and there are more dedicated politicians, more shades of political opinion and more political violence than most countries experience during a revolution. This, one might think, suits the Communist movement. But the electorate in 1972, rather than turn finally to Communism, turned back to Congress who chalked up their most impressive victory yet. The instability of West Bengal is not due to wilful exploitation by left wingers but to their own pitiful and helpless factionalism. For all the dedicated idealists and doctrinaire orators the basic problem is a conflict, not of ideologies but of factions and personalities. The same generalisation could be applied to the opposed wings of Congress or the Socialist parties. A Communist party is happier allied to a right-wing party than to another Communist faction. The vehement, sleepy-eyed idol of the C.P.M., Mr. Jyoti Basu, has more trouble defending his workers from the assaults of Naxalites on the one hand or from C.P.I. accusations of collusion with the Naxalites on the other than he does from the whole gamut of socialist, centrist, nationalist and rightist parties. It was this bitter struggle within the left which brought down the two United Front governments and had the whole state teetering on the brink of anarchy. Communism, like Christianity or Socialism, has been reduced to a very Indian plight where ideology is obscured by factionalism. The Victorian façades of Calcutta are splattered with hammers and sickles but no one seems to have bothered to rouse *en masse* the pavement dwellers and *basti* (shack) occupants who live beneath them. The Communists as much as anyone must respect caste sensibilities, as often as not the root cause of factionalism. So the bomb never went off. The Revolution never started and today it looks less likely than ever.

So much has been written about Calcutta* in recent years and so many people fly in and out of Dum Dum airport without seeing any more than the road to and from the city that one forgets that West Bengal, though industrialised by Indian standards, is still a predominantly rural state. At little country stations amid the rice fields or, farther north, the tea plantations, the hammer and sickle is still prevalent. The Naxalites were named not after some desperate Calcutta suburb but a pleasant village, Naxalbari, at the foot of the Himalayas where the first organised cell of agrarian revolutionaries was unearthed. Incidents of political violence reported by the newspapers invariably come from 24 Parganas, the half inundated area on the Bay of Bengal or from one of the small towns higher up the Hooghly river. As in Kerala, the seeds of revolution are sown amongst the tea pickers and paddy workers with a ready made grievance against the plantation owners and the Zamindars, the landowners of Bengal. Calcutta like Bombay was founded by the British. Even its substantial middle class has its roots in rural rather than urban Bengal. It is from the countryside of eastern India that Bengali culture, like Bengali politics, draws its inspiration.

Most of this lush scenery now falls in Bangladesh but there is sufficient in West Bengal to give some idea of its lyrical beauty. India embraces a scenic variety quite as complex and fascinating as its social composition. Compared to the grandeur of the Hima-

---

* For a full-length account of Calcutta as it is today see *Calcutta*, Geoffrey Moorhouse.

layas or the charm of the South, Bengal might not seem remark-able. Its big difference lies in a gentle homeliness and in the passionate attachment this has evoked in the Bengali people. The overall impression is of green luxuriance between well-kept, brown fields and beneath a deep blue sky. Water is abundant and the light has a special clarity without the harshness of a summer in the North or the haziness of a sunny day in Europe. Even in the hottest weather the air is moist and winter nights lack the pene-trating chill encountered in Delhi or the Punjab. The land is flat; shade and shelter are plentiful. In short it was and, in spite of typhoons and warfare, still is a good place to live. Not so long ago Bengal was known better for its prosperity than its poverty and the dangers of famine are more than matched by the land's natural resilience and abundance.

Noticeably absent is any sign of building stone. The Bengali builds out of mud and brick; there is little in the way of architec-tural tradition. Instead of statuary and temples the artistic genius of the Bengali was turned to music and literature. With the pos-sible exception of the South no region of India can claim such a rich heritage or flourishing contemporary culture.

Without a knowledge of the Bengali language or a real under-standing of Indian music it is impossible to do these justice. Some of Rabindranath Tagore's songs and poems were written in English or have been translated but one is always warned that to base any assessment of them on the English would be to do the Bengali Shakespeare a grave injustice. In the English-speaking world his poems became drawing-room *divertissements* of an innocuous character. One has only to witness a crowd of excited Bengalis chanting a bit of Tagore at a political meeting to realise that in translation something very odd must have happened. The crowd sways, the chant rises and falls and one is conscious of a passion and virility which would never have done at an Edwardian tea party. Imagery which in Bengali has a powerful magic, in English sounds contrived. Song after song evokes the Bengali countryside. For this Tagore has been called a nature poet but it is not pale daffodils or the gently rolling Cotswolds which he evokes. Rather it's a lush vibrant land whose very name, Bangla, is a rousing, resonant cry, a land not so much of hope and glory but of beauty and tragedy which fills its people not with loyalty and affection but with a fierce longing. I remember at the time of the Awami League's victory in East Bengal in 1970 a friend explaining its significance. 'The Bengali,' he said, 'is a Bengali first. After that he is a Hindu or a Muslim, an Indian or a Pakistani, a Communist or a right-winger, a man or a woman.' The same might be said of Sikhs, Tamils and other communities in India but the Bengalis are the only example of a people whose transcendent loyalty is not to a religion, language or caste but to their homeland.

Tagore's fame outside India has a lot to do with his being the first Asian to win a Nobel prize. This, together with the sheer stature of the man, poet, philosopher, musician and, inevitably, mystic, has won him a reputation of such eminence that other Indian, let alone Bengali, writers are easily overlooked. In fact Tagore was the flower of something called the Bengali Renaissance. From the mid-nineteenth century poets, playwrights, novelists and journalists began to experiment in Bengali with the forms and conventions of Western literature. Bengal had the longest and closest association with British rule. Education received a high priority. There was a sophisticated upper middle class and a language of more than adequate subtlety to take advantage of it. The result is Bengali literature, a true literary school, something to which no other modern Indian tongue can lay claim.

Of contemporary Bengali writers there is no shortage. The English newspapers from news to correspondence seem to be exclusively written by Roys and Rays, Mukherjis, Chatterjis and Bannerjis or Das(es) and Boses. For stylistic achievement coupled with a typically Bengali contentiousness one need look no further than the work of Nirad Chaudhuri.* Few English writers have such an understanding of their language yet too often Chaudhuri

---

* Author of *Diary of an Unknown Indian, Continent of Circe, Passage to England,* etc.

is wasting his delicate fastidious prose on imaginary critics. Every theme has to be justified, every omission explained and every slight anticipated. For the Bengali the pen is a sword and the spoken word a missile. Of subtlety there is plenty but it is the intensity one senses most.

The same could be said of Bengali music and cinema. Hard as it is for one who does not speak the language to appreciate Bengali literature, Indian music for any but the most tutored admirer is even more difficult. In the South music is closely connected with the dance, the Kathakali of Kerala or the Bharata Natyam of Tamil Nadu, both of which have a language and fascination of their own. It is possible to enjoy and even understand something of the music through the gestures and movements of the dance. But in Bengal and northern India as a whole Indian classical music—which is very rarely the noise which comes blaring from every transistor—is a distinct art form, immensely subtle, totally absorbing and, to me at least highly mysterious. Exciting and sensual it is quite free from the overpowering anguish and grandeur of Western music. Yet to a Bengali it is all and more than Wagner is to a Bayreuth audience. For as long as it would take to see the whole of The Ring cycle he will sit cross-legged and enraptured through an endless succession of *ragas*. Much will be improvisation but the conventions are such that the audience can revel in every development with the tense excitement of chess addicts following a match between Grand Masters.

More intelligible to most visitors is the movie. Predictably the only Indian director known outside Asia is another Bengali, Satyajit Ray. His, however, are not the films one sees advertised on every telegraph pole or hears announced from every bazaar loudspeaker. The idea of films as art is not widely appreciated in India. The movie makers in Bombay churn out a product of such horrifying quality, such insulting intelligence and such sickening conformity that one would expect Ray's films to have revolutionised the industry. In fact only in Bengal are they widely known and appreciated. Elsewhere, particularly in the South, a few sensitive and serious films are now appearing in the regional languages. And for the rest of the country it is still those four-hour Hindi travesties, beside which a Hollywood spectacular looks as coarsely realistic as a kitchen sink drama, which hold the national market in their oily grip. Apu, the hero of Ray's celebrated trilogy, is just an ordinary Bengali boy. There is no place for him amongst the Technicolor heroes with their rasping laments and swash-buckling exploits. It is, I suppose, an essential of the experience of India to see one of these Hindi films; but not something to be repeated.

★     ★     ★

Assam and the neighbouring hill states which form the rest of India's long and tortuous eastern frontier have little in common with West Bengal. Where the latter is now comparatively urbanised, industrialised, rich in culture and dominated by its middle class, Assam is still an unsophisticated, untamed land characterised by a largely tribal population and wildly beautiful scenery. Between the Assamese and the Bengalis there is as much simmering resentment as, in western India, between the Gujeratis and the Mahrattas. The Assamese feel that the Bengalis are exploiting them by dominating the bazaars and offices of Gauhati and Shillong. They want Assamese alone to be the official language. In 1969 and again in 1972 riots broke out between the native community and the Bengali-speaking settlers. Beneath the lin-guistic and economic clash lies the inevitable caste issue. The Bengalis are mainly Brahmins and invariably of higher caste than the humble, Untouchable or tribal Assamese.

Because of this unrest, because of the area's strategic importance and because alone in India it boasts oil resources, the central government treats Assam with great delicacy. To give as many as possible of the area's different communities a sense of participation in government and to ensure that their various needs and grie-vances are well aired a proliferation of states has come into existence; it makes the map of the region look like a patchwork quilt. In Andhra Pradesh there has for years been a strong and not unjustified movement in favour of dividing what is anyway a very large state.* The central government has resisted in spite of riots and bloodshed but in Assam with little or no prompting another new state was born in 1972. There are now six. Assam proper, that is the Brahmaputra valley, Meghalaya, the hill districts to the south, Arunachal Pradesh, those to the north, Nagaland, home of the restive Naga tribesmen, Manipur and Tripura, both one-time princely states. The visitor is normally granted access only to the first two, the others being too strategically important or politically sensitive. Of the colourful Manipuris or the head-hunting Nagas it is difficult to gain any first-hand knowledge. Instead one comes away with a taste of the burgeoning officialdom and bureaucracy resulting from the recognition of so many small states. The governor in Shillong doubles for several states but each has its own assembly and its own state government.

At Gauhati our arrival coincided with the local Congress parties' conference. Both rest houses, the main hotel and the club were full of ministers. By the time we reached Karen Lodgings both we and our rickshaw cyclist were exhausted. We struggled up the stone stairs to a reception desk tucked away on the second floor. Amidst the odd assortment of tickets and addresses one accumulates when travelling I still have the card of Karen Lodgings. It sounds promising.

Municipal Award Winners for neat and best premises. Solicit your in-estimable co-operation with family and friends. A palace for your comfort with modern facilities! Noble service!! Delicious dishes to choice!!! A warm welcome!!!!

'A warm welcome,' said the bespectacled old man behind the desk and went on counting an enormous bundle of notes.

'Thank you, but have you a room?'

Yes there was a room, just one of the seventy shown on the key board was not occupied by an M.P. But there was no attached

* In late 1972 there was more rioting over the 'Telengana' controversy. Andhra consists of backward areas previously part of the Nizam of Hyderabad's state and more prosperous areas in the south and east. Both are Telugu-speaking but the difference in economic conditions necessitates an invidious allocation of job opportunities and development projects.

bath. Did we mind a shared bath? Had we, I asked, any choice? Every hotel was full. That was true but still, did we mind? In any case we must first see the room. It was a small bare cell. Round its dazzling strip light the ceiling was alive with insects and the only window opened straight into the shared bath. It was hot and airless.

'How about a cold drink?'

Not possible; the delegates had polished them off to the last soda water. Tea? 'Noble Service' in the shape of a young man in just a *lungi* set off saying it might take a little time. We were left to deal with the rickshaw wallah who with one foot in the door was demanding ten rupees to the four I offered. A splitting headache and the opening skirmishes of what promised to be a long, net-less battle with the mosquitoes found me shorter than usual. I thrust five rupees under his turban and slammed the door.

Thirty minutes later after an unhappy acquaintance with the shared bath there was still no sign of Noble Service. The rickshaw man was still there. Although in one piece the note I had given him was too old. At great length the old man at the desk explained how in the bazaar no one would accept this note so how was the poor rickshaw man to buy his provisions. My patience was exhausted. The note fluttered back and forth as the old man stuck it into my breast pocket and I thrust it back at the rickshaw wallah's turban. I remember shouting

'Is it or is it not valid? Doesn't it say "I promise to pay the bearer the sum of five rupees?" It's your currency, not mine. You ought to know. And where the hell is that tea?'

'No tea, all finished. It is Congress Party Conference.'

It was a bad moment. India has a positive genius for souring the sweetest of tempers and mine was never that.

'Assam,' I screamed, 'Assam, the Mecca of the tea industry, and you tell me you haven't any. Pick some.'

I was beginning to understand why the tourist department tend to discourage visitors from travelling east of Bengal. Their explanation of a shortage of adequate accommodation began to make sense.

Fortunately this experience, which in one form or another is the lot of every visitor to India, is not peculiar to Assam nor even particularly typical of the area. Beyond Gauhati one enters a land of enchantment more like South-East Asia than India. In Rajasthan the deserts of the East encroach and in neighbouring Gujarat there are lions, African Negroes and Arab princes, but here the palm groves give way to bamboo thickets and the sari to the sarong. The jungle grows thicker and edges nearer the Brahmaputra. The paddy fields are more steeply terraced and over the densely wooded mountains hangs a deep blue haze. The villagers are not the sleek Bengalis or the bony Biharis but neat, pale-skinned tribals with the flat, smiling and much-creased faces of an un-mistakably Mongolian people.

If the Assamese are suspicious and resentful of their neighbours they have considerably more justification than most. Until 1826 they were independent. While Bengal was an integral part of every Indian empire from Ashoka onwards Assam managed to defy even the Moghuls. From the thirteenth to the nineteenth centuries the Ahom kings (hence the name 'Assam') ruled the Brahmaputra valley and maintained as close a contact with Burma, their land of origin, as they did with Bengal and India. They were finally overcome not by Indian forces but by the Burmese and it was only after the British subjugation of Burma that Assam became part of the Indian Empire.

Indians as a whole are notoriously ignorant about the area. Mahatma Gandhi has never been forgiven for classing the Assamese tribals with the aboriginal Bhils and Santhals of central India. There are indeed a few remarkably primitive peoples. The Apa Tanis of Arunachal Pradesh wear stiff red tails curling down to the backs of their knees. But these are the exceptions. The Assamese, according to Murray's 1882 *Handbook*, are 'proud, haughty and indolent and use opium to an injurious extent'. Tribals like the Khasis, Jantias, Mikirs and Manipuris are certainly not aboriginal. As in the Himalayas a society based on the tribe rather than caste is a product of geographical isolation rather than some primitive totemism.

The two facts about Assam which every guide book or tourist brochure reiterates are that Cherrapunji has the heaviest rainfall in the world and that Kaziranga is the last remaining haunt of the Indian rhinoceros—evidence enough if more were needed that the region's character is of a natural rather than a civilised or social order. Four hundred and twenty-six inches is the average annual total at Cherrapunji but in 1861 it apparently reached an incredible nine hundred and six inches. Nearly all of this falls, as everywhere in India except the extreme south and Kashmir, during the monsoon months of June to September. Like Durga and Kali the monsoon has its destructive as well as its beneficial aspect. Throughout India a period of intense anxiety precedes the annual *Götterdämmerung*. By the middle of June everyone hopes to be somewhere safe and comfortable. From Bombay the construction workers head for their villages, the princely M.P.s jet off for a bout of socialising overseas and the Delhi diplomats pack their wives and children off to Kashmir. Parliament and the state assemblies go into recess. For three months the country is at a standstill. Train services are disrupted, villages are cut off, power supplies fail. In the palace hotels they roll up the carpets and store them in a dry room. At the old British clubs a fire has to be lit under the billiard tables to counteract the damp, but in their neglected libraries ancient volumes of *Punch* and *Pall Mall* rot with mildew. Fields and gardens are washed away, mud houses crumble and thatched hutments collapse. And all this in just an average, a good monsoon.

It is difficult to gauge the effect of the monsoon on the Indian mentality. Often it is said that the country's climate is largely responsible for the fatalism ascribed to Indians. The idea of a supine race submitting placidly to perpetual poverty, conquest and social discrimination is too well attested to need emphasising. But that the resignation of the Indian peasant is the result of centuries of toil in the relentless heat interspersed by helpless anxiety occasioned by the annual rains seems doubtful. The dictates of caste *dharma*, the doctrines of reincarnation and *ahimsa*, the persistence of the family household and so on would appear to have more direct bearing on this phenomenon. Not all monsoon peoples are submissive, nor indeed are all Indians. The Sikhs, for example, with a climate in Punjab not so different from that of the rest of Northern India, are far from being fatalists. The reason lies not in the weather but in their religion.

If there is an Indian response to the monsoon it is to be found in the respect felt by Indians for their environment. The tension as the clouds build up and the heat increases communicates itself to man and beast. Even in the cities the streets are deserted; everyone seems to be under the spell of some psychological preoccupation. Then with startling regularity the first storms break amidst peals of thunder. The clouds roll across Bengal getting trapped by the hills around Cherrapunji or deflected west to continue their slow progress up through Bihar to U.P. In their wake first the insect world, then crops, plants and trees jerk into life. It's not the slow regeneration of a Northern spring but a sudden explosion of life. After the first deluge the clouds roll on; there may be days, even weeks, of tantalising waiting before the next downpour. Or the rain may fall incessantly flooding fields, streets, villages and roads. One wonders will it ever stop or is this perhaps the end of the world. You feel part of nature in a way that would seem absurd to the gardener or farmer in the West, who understands only how to exploit her generosity. Amidst the anxiety and excitement there is the joy of feeling at one with all that is happening and, as the farmer reconstructs his terraced fields or thrusts into the warm mud to plant his rice crop, of contributing to it. Participation with the forces of nature, rather than resignation in the face of them, is a more typically Indian attitude.

As uniquely Indian as the relationship between man and nature is that between man and beast. John Lockwood Kipling, Rudyard's father, wrote a book★ on the subject which in its way is as entertaining and revealing about India as anything written by his son. Besides the cow and other bovines, the peacock, monkey, elephant and snake are all to some degree holy. The elephant's head is that belonging to the jovial god, Ganesh. The peacock is

★ *Beast and Man in India.*

the chariot of Saraswati, the goddess of learning and the snake that of Vishnu. The monkey god is Hanuman. When the British were dubbed 'the monkey army' they failed to appreciate the honour implied in being named after this great warrior. Many other animals enjoy important roles in Indian mythology but all beasts, birds and insects are, according to Hindu, Jain and Buddhist belief, entitled to toleration. The parrot sitting in his cage on the balcony may well have been a distant relative in his last incarnation. Even the Brahmin high up the ladder of caste may slip down the snake of *karma* to reappear as a lowly cockroach. The animal kingdom is not something separate but as much part of the whole hierarchy of life as the Untouchable castes or the unclean foreigners. The distant but tolerant attitude shown to them extends to the animals. As a result nowhere in the world are monkeys so mischievous or birds so tame.

Most visitors prepared to face the skirmish involved in getting a travel permit for Assam head for the game reserve of Kaziranga. This is the most famous sanctuary in Asia. On elephant-back in the first light of day—particularly early in Assam—one watches the Great One-horned Indian rhinoceros, a prehistoric armour-plated monster, browsing and snorting in the open grassland with the morning mists swirling round him. Like that trip down the Ganges as the sun rises opposite Benares it's a moving, elemental experience, the first minutes of daybreak somehow capturing the timeless, changeless nature of a primeval world. This is a feeling which haunts one throughout rural India. So little seems to have changed. The plough is the same as in Vedic times, the fishermen cast their nets as they did at Galilee and the *saddhu* covered in ashes could be wearing woad. To me this contact with the uncivilised past is more exciting even than the beauty of the Taj or the abandon of Vijayanagar. That a world of simple pursuits and primal obligations should still exist or that the society of tribal peoples and primitive beliefs should still prosper, is cause not so much for shame but, in this age of conservation awareness, a degree of respect.

The wild life sanctuaries of India are a far cry from the game parks of Africa. There are no zebra-striped minibuses and as yet their attraction for the visitor is not fully appreciated by the authorities. Often they are almost inaccessible. After a formidable journey one is liable to arrive and find that there is no accommodation. Provided, however, that the wild life is there this absence of facilities and people is not so regrettable. At Periyar Lake in the Cardamom Hills of Kerala we completed a twelve-hour journey with a short boat trip to a remote rest house. The *chaukidar*, caretaker and general factotum, greeted us by asking whether we had seen the herd of elephants. He pointed at where we had just landed but there was nothing. What a pity, they must have moved off as we approached. But I was sceptical and when he indicated some distant shapes on the other side of the lake saying they were bison they could just as well have been cows. Before sunset we walked off into the woods to see for ourselves. The enormous dead leaves of the teak trees crackled under foot like crisp pappadums and the elephant grass was so high one could rarely see over it. We headed for the *machan*, a raised lookout hut, but just as we approached an enormous rock on the other side of it moved. I peered round. Less than ten yards away there were eight of these big grey rocks, all moving, all elephants. We crawled to the *machan*, the elephants held their ground and continued tearing up trunkfuls of grass or gingerly picking shoots off a bush. Only as they moved quietly away, gliding through the grass with long leisurely pauses, was I really impressed. Such grace and freedom was personified, such a sense of belonging to and possessing the countryside. There was no sign of fear and no suggestion of the grotesque. They were wild all right yet they were tame.

In the days that followed we spent a lot of time following herds like this on foot through the woods and grassland. It's quite different to spying animals from a boat or a car. You move cautiously, stopping frequently to listen and look. You learn something of the animals' way of life and you respect their conventions about being silent and wary. All the time I felt I was being privileged to see something very special, a bit of the world as it was meant to be, totally unselfconscious. The feeling grew on me. We were watching a herd of wild boar when suddenly they scattered for cover. Immediately and silently there trotted into the clearing a gigantic bull bison.* His horns shone in the sun and the strong neck was stiff beneath thick hair. Then with a great sense of power he moved slowly across our path and up into the long grass. The thrill was of being there on equal terms with him and, because he neither fled nor charged, of feeling accepted.

This sense of being accepted as an equal, or at least as someone whose presence is not resented, is what the visitor or traveller most likes to feel. It is possibly the most rewarding part of the experience of India. In the cities you are still over-charged by shopkeepers, cheated by taxi-drivers, mobbed by students and questioned unmercifully by everyone. But rarely if ever are you actually resented and just occasionally you feel quietly, genuinely accepted. For a while people will stare as you sit at the village tea-shop or climb into the railway carriage. A few polite questions will be asked and someone will make a joke about your shoes or your hair. Given just a smattering of Hindi or someone who understands English you are drawn into the conversation and become part of a little world which would not have been so different if you hadn't been there. To share a place, a moment with a very different people occasions for me the same excitement, the same sense of being privileged to be there as when following the elephants.

Kaziranga sanctuary, besides its rhinos, boasts a few tigers. Seven according to the census officer. The tiger needs a lot of territory; he may cover fifty miles in a night. All over India the tiger population is in a bad way. At the Gir forest in Gujerat the Indian lion population is down to a pathetic, semi-tame quota of about two hundred beasts living in an environment not much more natural than Longleat. The tiger has not yet sunk quite so low but he is still a very rare and threatened species. One does not expect to see one even in a sanctuary. By rights we should there-fore have been overwhelmed when on that same morning with

* The Indian 'gaur'. No relation to the bison of North America and properly an ox rather than a bison.

the rhinos browsing in the mist, our elephant suddenly reared back and thumped the ground with his trunk as one of these majestic creatures looked disdainfully over his shoulder and slunk casually off into the woods. It was the sort of event that should make one's trip to India. Yet somehow it did not seem in the least bit exceptional. If there are seven tigers in Kaziranga's three hundred square miles, why not?

Even a few weeks in India has a way of closing one's credibility gap. The improbable becomes the commonplace and the fantastic just the noteworthy. Charmed snakes, dancing bears and yogis on their nail beds are the obvious manifestations of a phenomenon which extends to the whole of Indian life. Gullibility is a national trait but the tallest story is not to be dismissed outright. The toleration and acceptance which India extends to everyone and everything are contagious. One still seethes at every instance of petty officialdom and bridles at every bit of obstructive mismanagement yet at the same time one learns to expect it. A simple concurrence with what the slings and arrows have in store is the only way in India. It is not hopeless resignation; more just an easy going open-mindedness.

# 8. A NOT SO DIFFERENT WORLD

## Kashmir and the Himalayas

The Himalayas besides being the highest mountains in the world are also the newest. Like the wayward course of the Ganges their geography is still in the making. Rumbling avalanches, crumbling hill-sides, edging glaciers and rivers impetuous with melted snow give any journey into the 'hills' a touch of pioneering excitement. Leaving the cosy familiarity and the steady rhythm of the broad-gauge system you embark at Pathankot, Kalka, Raxaul or Siliguri for a battered little bus or a narrow-gauge toy train for the climb to Kashmir, Simla, Kathmandu or Darjeeling. The excitement is intense. Wiry little hillmen swarm over the luggage being piled on the roof of the bus. A dashing Nepali sporting a badge of King Mahendra,* or a heavily built Sardarji twirling his moustache slides in behind the wheel. After several false starts the bus lurches off. The seemingly impenetrable barrier of mountains rearing up along the northern horizon reminds one of the cool fresh air, of green pastures and coniferous forests. It seems incredible but in a couple of hours the stifling heat, parched soil and suffocating dust are forgotten. The smell of cow dung gives way to the resinous pine and the creaking ox-cart is superseded by the crisp clip-clop of ponies and the distant tolling of cow-bells. Every sound and smell is as hard and sharp as the mountain contours. Huddled in their seats, swathed in scarves and shawls, the visitors from the plains look apprehensively through closed windows at the sheer drop while the hillmen gaze happily ahead to the misty peaks.

The hairpin bends grow sharper, the air keener and the forests thicker. 'You are at 2,000 metres above sea level' proclaims a road sign, and the posters for family planning—'You have two, that

* King of Nepal. He died in 1972 to be succeeded by his son King Birendra.

will do'—and forestry conservation—'Nature's most beautiful poem, a tree'—give way to 'Safety Saves' and 'Overtaker-Undertaker'. The bus fills with fumes as the engine grows hotter and the gear-box noisier. At a wayside shrine there's a brief stop. The radiator is filled from a spring. In return for a quickly made collection of small change the old saddhu who lives in the shrine provides a couple of joss sticks for safe passage over the pass. Off again, this time into the mists with the big trees dripping silently and road gangs from the P.W.D. (Public Works Department) repairing the damage of recurrent landslides. The chipping of their hammers echoes through the mist from some invisible hill-side while far below there is the roar of a frantic river.

If your destination is Kashmir the pass is the long and gloomy Banihal tunnel. The bus trundles down it as if hell-bent for Hades. The darkness reverberates to the thunder of military convoys and water cascades out of the murk to drum on the roof and luggage. The pale light of a new day and a new world filters through and in a matter of seconds not hell but 'Paradise on Earth', the most beautiful valley of Kashmir, stretches out below. It was the Moghul emperor Jehangir who called it that and somewhere east of the Banihal *en route* to the valley he died. 'Was there anything he wanted?' they asked as he lay on his deathbed. 'Only Kashmir' came the faint reply as he passed away, baulked of one paradise and none too promising a candidate for the next.

Much the same attachment to Kashmir might be credited to Pandit Nehru who, himself of Kashmiri Brahmin descent, presided over Kashmir's accession to India and was prepared to defy even the United Nations over it. Or of his successor, Lal Bahadur Shastri, who died a matter of hours after signing the Tashkent agreement which in effect recognised the partition of the state. The same too could be said of all of Pakistan's leaders since Independence. Everyone wants Kashmir. Without going into the rights and wrongs of a dispute which has governed the whole course of the subcontinent's politics in the last quarter century it can safely be said that Kashmir's significance is not simply that of any Indian state. Like Bengal and Assam its strategic importance

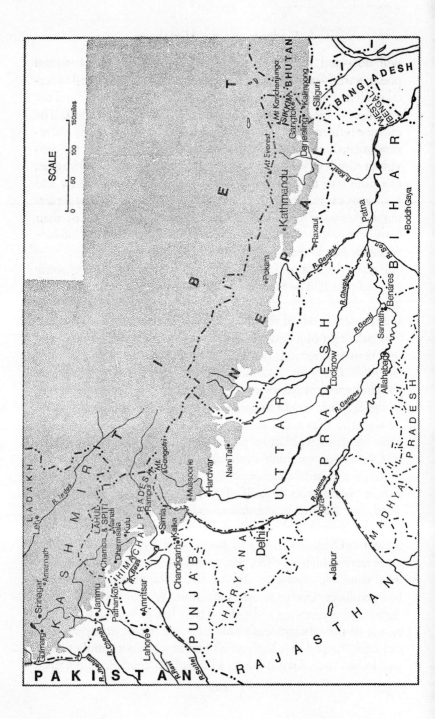

is tremendous. Tibet, Sinkiang, Afghanistan and, but for a neck of glaciers, Russia have common frontiers with Kashmir. But even this hardly accounts for the intensity of feeling which Kashmir arouses on both sides. Kashmir, the state,* is a land of staggering mountains, an oyster cradling the 'pearl of Asia', the Kashmir valley, the largest and richest in the Himalayas, with its soil watered by countless mountain streams, shaded by glorious trees and dotted with azure lakes. Though populated by a weak and ineffectual race, Kashmir has been loved with a fierce passion by the succession of invaders and visitors who thought of it as theirs.

To the Pakistani it is the home of intensely orthodox fellow Muslims who constitute seventy per cent of the population. It houses a celebrated relic, a hair of the Prophet's beard, and was the playground of the Moghuls. To the Hindu it is the home of the highly respected pandits, Brahmin teachers, the land of snows and the abode of gods, a place for pilgrimage, particularly to the famous cave of Amarnath, and the source of saffron, that most sacred of crops as vital in cooking and religious ceremony as it is in dyeing the saddhu's robes. Punjab and Bengal were divided but Kashmir is not so easily carved up. The oyster may be split but the pearl, the valley itself, is too small and too precious. Indians speak of Kashmir as might an Englishman of the Highlands or a New Yorker of California. It represents a vital feature of the national consciousness, remote but, as anything other than a part of India, unthinkable.

There is a Persian saying which runs to the effect that if the world is coming to an end on no account choose as father of a new race either a Pathan† or 'the rascally Kashmiri'. The poor Kashmiris, no one has ever had a good word for them. Fairer than most Indians—even red hair is not uncommon—they have been thought to be descendants of the lost tribe of Israelites or of Alexander the Great's Greeks. Such hypotheses have been

---

* The Indian state of Kashmir is properly 'Jammu and Kashmir'. It includes Ladakh' the valley of Kashmir and the foothills around the town of Jammu. Most of the north and west of what was Kashmir is now administered by Pakistan.

† The warrior tribesmen of the north-west Frontier, now part of Pakistan, and of Afghanistan.

summarily dismissed by anyone with a closer knowledge of the Kashmiri character. Though charm, wit and a certain arrogance are there the national trait is, undeniably, dishonesty. Even the fair-minded British Sahibs never quite recovered from the shock of finding such a perfect land inhabited by such an untrustworthy, spineless and obtuse people. After the Sikh wars in which the British acquired most of Ranjit Singh's empire in north-west India they sold Kashmir for a mere seven-and-a-half million rupees. The arrangement saved the Raj the problem of administering such a corrupt and remote people but ensured that the enervated sahibs could visit the area for relaxation and sport.

This they did in ever-increasing numbers. The Moghuls had endowed the valley with their own very Persian ideas of luxury in the form of ornamental gardens like Shalimar and Nishat. Their idea of the good life was to loll in the midst of court and harem beside a tinkling water course among the flower-beds. The chutes and the fountains were designed to produce a harmony of watery noises and the flowers so planted that their different scents blended happily. Life beneath the giant *chenar* trees was a sensuous and delicate affair. British visitors respected the horticulture but despised the indolence. Their contribution was to stock the streams with brown trout from Scotland, to turn the beautiful meadows of Gulmarg into a golf course and to dot the hill sides with Rest Houses for the weary sportsmen. Base camp was usually a houseboat—by law only Kashmiris can own land in Kashmir— on one of the lakes round Srinagar, the capital. Like floating cricket pavilions they were built in the grand style and furnished with chintz-covered armchairs, mahogany dining-tables and flushing lavatories.

From the traditional Kashmiri professions of farming, trading and carpet manufacture many turned to what is now the tourist industry. On the houseboats the cook will still be a dab hand at dropscones or bread and butter pudding; if you ask for something local, perhaps a curry, he knows that what you mean is not a Kashmiri delicacy like lotus stalks in yogurt but the chops, which you were going to get anyway, cooked in a thick yellow concoction from a tin labelled 'curry powder'.* The manufacture of papiermâché cigarette boxes, walnut coffee tables and sheepskin jackets along with the more traditional arts of shawl and carpet weaving have created a highly tourist-orientated economy.

Any fall in quality occasioned by large-scale production is counteracted by the Kashmiri's exceptional ability as a salesman. The Kashmir Arts Emporium is a feature of every Indian city from Trivandrum to Darjeeling. Inside there are always the same two figures, a slim, angular young man with a pale complexion and an older, heavily built gentleman bent over the books. They speak excellent English (in Kashmir it is still the official language) and have a good grasp of foreign exchange rates. Somehow they always gauge the extent of your interest. They have an uncanny knack of drawing it from the cheap trinkets on the shelves to some antique of considerable value which is locked away at the back of the shop.

It is ironic that the money-loving Kashmiri should be in the middle of the bitterest quarrel on the subcontinent. Their history is the story of successive invasions rarely resisted; by the British only the Bengali was considered less martial. While India and Pakistan have argued and fought over the region's status the Kashmiris have done precious little about it. Every incident of violence means a slackening in the tourist trade and is therefore resented by the wealthy shopkeepers of Srinagar.

Cheap John, the tailor, or Suffering Moses, the curio king—like the Parsis Kashmiris appreciate the value to their trade of an easily remembered name—are reportedly generous in their donaions to political organisations. The Plebiscite Front is said to be the main recipient. This party has for years spear-headed Kashmiri resentment over the method of the state's incorporation into India. It maintains that the plebiscite urged by the United Nations as an equable way of deciding Kashmir's position on the subcontinent has never been held. Although banned by the Indian government it has shown by support of the occasional independent candidate that its appeal is still strong. Sheikh Abdullah, its ageing leader

---

* Curry powder was devised for European palates and has no place in Indian cuisine.

dubbed 'The Lion of Kashmir', is still, in spite of long prison sentences and externment orders, the most widely respected political figure in the state. His triumphal return after another long sojourn under house arrest in Delhi or Bombay is like a royal progress down the valley. But all the flag waving and tub thumping, which are avidly magnified by the Pakistani press, have little effect. If there is an outbreak of violence it is usually some splinter group or extremist faction which claims responsibility. The Plebiscite Front has never come out in favour of secession from India and has never condoned armed resistance or violent agitation. Suffering Moses and the rest are too shrewd to finance anyone whose activities are likely to prejudice their trade.

On a Friday in October when the tourists have begun to thin out but before the long cold winter sets in, Kashmiri Muslims congregate at the Hazratbal mosque outside Srinagar. All day the road from the city throbs with buses and pony carts as close on a quarter of a million people make for the sacred shrine. The occasion is the public exposition of the Prophet's Hair, one solitary hair from Mohammed's beard, which is the valley's most cherished relic. In 1956 it was the disappearance of this relic which occasioned the worst riots the valley has ever known. It took a sacrilege like the discovery of a page of the Koran down one of the University's lavatories to produce, ten years later, a public reaction of comparable gravity.

The mosque is quite unlike a temple in that it is a political as well as a religious and social centre. In the whole of the vast temple complex at Madurai there is no open arena where you could address more than a few hundred people. But at any mosque there is invariably a vast forecourt, often enlarged as at Hazratbal by the surrounding gardens and lawns. The focus of the place is not an altar or an idol but, at Hazratbal, a platform studded with microphones. And as the highlight of the occasion the exposition of the sacred hair is almost overshadowed by the speech from Sheikh Sahib (Sheikh Abdullah). In the Islamic world church and state are one. The mosque is invariably the centre of political intrigue and there is nothing like a religious issue for rousing the faithful to political protest. In this the orthodox Kashmiris and their mullahs are no exception. But it says as much for the Indian handling of the situation as for the timidity or commonsense of the Kashmiri that every year this vast and often excitable gathering has passed off without any hostile outbreaks.

If the visitor to Kashmir encounters resentment it is rarely against Indian rule as opposed to Pakistani but an Indian presence as opposed to a British one. Although Kashmir was never part of British India it owed more to the Raj than many parts that were. The state was surveyed by British engineers and the fairest land settlement ever drawn up was the work of a British administrator; it is remembered to this day. But the real bond was one of money. The sahibs and their families turned Kashmir into a rich man's playground. A whole new suburb of Srinagar grew up round the alien's holiday requirements, photographic shops, *shikar*★ outfitters, tinned-food suppliers, trout-fly manufacturers. At Gulmarg a holiday town sprang up round the golf course. St. Mary's church, built in stone, stands in the middle; scattered between the fairways are hotels˙and clubs with, round the perimeter of the course, elaborate wooden houses, all gables, balconies, dormer windows and loggias. In those days there was no road up from the valley; supplies, furnishings, even people were carried up the 3,000 feet. Thousands of visitors spent the whole summer presenting their cards and galloping up to the glaciers to clear their heads in the morning.

Now things are different. My Urdu teacher in Srinagar carried a wallet of letters from long-departed subalterns expressing appreciation of his teaching. Munshi Gopi Nath had seen them through the Hindustani Intermediate with flying colours; I was not to be discouraged by his bad breath and on no account to countenance a demand for a higher hourly fee once I had mastered declension. Actually the demand came much sooner and, when it did, I gave in. Apart from a Swedish colonel working with the U.N. peace-keeping force, I was his first pupil for fifteen years. Munshi used to spend the summers up at Gulmarg with his pupils

★ Hunting or shooting.

but he does not go there now. It's a ghostly place with garden gates swinging in the cold wind that sweeps down from the glaciers. Each winter another dormer collapses under the weight of snow and sheep shelter in the porch of St. Mary's. The tourist authorities have turned it into a ski resort but a winter holiday at over 8,000 feet appeals little to Indians.

Munshi is a Brahmin like most Kashmiri Hindus; other castes are rare in the valley. Representative of the Muslims, here the majority community, is Ghulam Mohammed. He distrusts Munshi intensely but not primarily because the latter is Hindu. All Kashmiris, regardless of religion, distrust one another. A more suspicious people it is hard to imagine. Ghulam Mohammed insists that only an Englishman can be trusted. He is an old man, thin but still erect. He wears the traditional Kashmiri dress of astrakhan (Persian lamb) hat, *pheron* (a voluminous tent-shaped garment with baggy sleeves) and shapeless trousers. During the cold winter evenings he crouches on the floor with a *kangri*, a clay-lined basket full of burning charcoal, tucked inside his *pheron*. Primed with a cigarette or a glass of whisky he will talk for hours.

'Sahib, you are like son to me. I tell you everything. Today I buy firewood. Forty rupees a maund. British times it was ten. Why these people want so much money? You know Kashmiri people. Kashmiri people not interested war, fighting. Enough trouble to stop kangri putting light to pheron. British times many sahibs come to Kashmir. Kashmir people happy. Now Indian people come, very dirty, eating this cow's mess, no bath. Sahib I tell you these people not know how to live. Kashmiri rice, Kashmiri firewood goes to military. Everything very expensive. This rice I give you must come from Punjab.

'What to do? Sheikh Sahib [Sheikh Abdullah] in Delhi. Congress say Kashmir Indian, Pakistan radio say Kashmir in Pakistan. Kashmiri people not happy. British sahibs must come back. This Attlee, why he do this thing?* Churchill sahib should have stopped him.'

* Attlee was the British Prime Minister responsible for conceding India's independence. Churchill always disapproved of it.

In fairness it must be said that India has done a great deal for Kashmir. There are new universities, hydro-electric schemes and tourist projects. Inflation is no worse here than elsewhere. The sahibs were in the enviable position of patrons rather than rulers; responsibility for domestic affairs was the Maharajah's. But however significant Kashmir is in the eyes of India, Kashmiris do not regard themselves as Indians. A Bengali or a Tamil will never talk of 'Indians' as a foreign people though he may hesitate before describing himself as one. But for the Kashmiri there is the Banihal Pass and the Pir Panjal range dividing him from India. Indians begin at Jammu just as Europeans, to an Englishman, begin at Calais.

This sense of being other than Indian is common to most of the Himalayan peoples. Locked in their remote valleys, spared the continuous invasions which have shaped the history of the plains and divided even from their neighbours by differences of race, language and religion each can claim the same degree of independence from the life of the subcontinent. The Himalayas are not simply one of the world's great natural frontiers. So vast is their scale and so many are the inhabited valleys and plateaux that they may be regarded as a distinct social region. Here, not over a well-defined ridge but in countless valleys and grazing grounds, the Buddhist, Hindu and Islamic worlds meet. Aryan features shade through a variety of combinations into the purely Mongol; language, customs and dress evidence the same transition. But however little the people may regard themselves as Indians the visitors' experience of Himalayan society is not unlike that of Indian society as a whole. Just as at Bombay airport or Old Delhi station one may sit and witness the extraordinary variety of Indian types, so at any bazaar in the Himalayas one may observe a similar diversity amongst the peoples of the hills. If anything the differences are even more marked. Yet as in the plains and in the South widely different communities, though rarely blending together, seem happily to co-exist. Even in Kashmir communal strife between Muslim and Hindu Kashmiris is a rare occurrence.

In the four winter months of December to March most of the

Himalayan passes are closed, the rich grazing on the high alps is deep in snow and road gangs, porters and muleteers retreat to their villages or to the foothills. But in April the snow line recedes up the slopes and the trek back into the mountains begins. Activity in roadhead and railhead bazaars is intense as the hill people set off and the first tourists start to arrive. On the road up to Kashmir herds of long-haired goats and sturdy little sheep bring the traffic to a standstill. Their wild-looking herdsmen who, with women, children, donkeys and mules, add to the confusion, are the Gujars. From Nepal in the east to Afghanistan in the west these tall, imposing people range through the western Himalayas. On the higher pastures they may have constructed a rough hut but most of the year they live in tents. In Himachal Pradesh buffaloes rather than goats are their stock, but as in Kashmir they are nomads and Muslims to a man. Their origin is something of a mystery. In the plains the term Gujar is applied to a race or caste of herdsmen but these are invariably Hindus. The names of many quite orthodox subcastes include the word and the state of Gujerat and the town of Gujranwala in Pakistan, are clearly derived from the same source. Perhaps like the Rajputs they, too, are the dismembered remnants of some once great people. There is a pride in their bearing and a classical beauty in their women which belies their dirty clothes and untidy turbans.

Farther east the same season sees the Ghaddi shepherds heading up through the valleys of Chamba and Kulu (Himachal Pradesh). Though sharing the high pastures with the Gujars they could hardly be more different. Short and stocky, dressed in rough tweed jackets, skirts and small pillbox hats, all of a natural colour, they are practically indistinguishable from their flocks. The jackets are buttonless but belted, from the pouch above the belt the head of a new-born lamb looks out. Over their backs are slung a few warm rugs, also undyed, and a bag of flour. Beneath their skirts hangs a pouch with tinder-box, tobacco and pipe. For the long summer months ahead these are their only provisions. To reach the best pastures at 12,000–15,000 feet in Lahul they must be able to travel fast and sleep rough. Unlike the Gujars they have a home and a village to look forward to. Their vast flocks of up to a thousand beasts represent the combined resources of several villages in their native region of Kangra or Brahmaur. By October they will be heading home again with flocks heavier for the good grass and bigger for the new lambs—assuming, that is, that the gods are kind to them. The Ghaddis are nominally Hindus but like most of the hill people their gods are not so much Vishnu and Siva as the spirits of the passes and the deities of woods and rocks.

Below in the bazaars of Kulu and Simla the Lahuli muleteers are loading up their beasts for the first trip north to Lahul, Spiti and Ladakh. Once over the Rohtang Pass they enter a rugged, barren land, the Indian Tibet, where the focus of society is the Buddhist monastery and the language a dialect of Bhoti, the Tibetan tongue. The Lahuli men themselves have the straight hair and a hint of the high cheekbones of a Mongol. Their women, doe-eyed and demure, wear a distinctive long dress of black or brown velvet with braided border and matching waistcoat. Their hair is in a long pigtail with perhaps a ribbon of bright pink to match the sash round their waists.

Jostling with them outside the dry goods store with its sacks of flour, rice, millet and spices is a red-robed lama from Ladakh still wearing his tall hat with flaps upturned like horns. No doubt he is returning, like Kim's friend, from a tour of the Buddhist shrines at Gaya, Benares and Sanchi. Fellow Ladakhis, the finest high altitude porters in the western Himalayas, are sporting the anoraks given them by last year's climbers as they hang round the tea shops waiting for the first of this year's expeditions. They look as effete as coffee-bar cowboys but the frailest will soon be shouldering a forty-pound pack and cutting steps in the ice at 20,000 feet.

Heading north with the mountainfolk and muleteers come the birds, beautiful scarlet minivets and blue flycatchers. They flit through the orchards of the Beas and Sutlej valleys, now white with blossom rather than snow. From the long winter of spinning and weaving the local Pahari-speaking population emerge; contact is re-established with the remote side valleys of Pangi, Malana and

Bara Bangahal. The village deities are paraded up and down the steep tracks to the accompaniment of flute and drums and the first *melas*, village fairs, get under way. Throughout the summer this feting of the gods continues, culminating in the great Dussehra celebration on the maidan, a sort of village green, at Kulu.

One learns to avoid long bus journeys in India. It's a forty-hour nightmare of hazards and hairpins from Srinagar to Kulu but to get from the excitements of Hazratbal to Kulu in time for the climax of the week of festivities we had no choice. As the little bus struggled up the last hundred feet on to the maidan I could wiggle every tooth so loose had they become from the incessant vibration. Paralysis from the waist down had us reeling out of the wooden seats and into the festive crowds like a pair of boozy party goers.

Dussehra is a Hindu festival sacred to the goddess Durga. Elsewhere in India, and particularly in Mysore city, it is a great occasion overshadowed only by the celebration, a few weeks later, of Divali. In Kulu it is more important than Divali though Durga scarcely gets a look in. There are enough deities on the upper Beas without importing the whole of the Hindu pantheon.* And the Dussehra festival though one of the greatest social events for the peoples of the western Himalayas is essentially a get-together of gods; every village has at least one. As gods go these are some of the most human. Sitting on a palanquin in his tent or going the rounds of his neighbours at the fair, each god may not look particularly manlike—just a collection of gold and silver masks reclining on a bed of brightly coloured silks and perhaps shaded by a parasol. But appearances can be deceptive. The gods and goddesses of Kulu expect regular meals, occasional baths and constant attention. Some, even, are landowners, subject to the land ceiling and not averse to a bit of litigation.

Dussehra is traditionally the occasion for the paying of respects to Ragunathji, the host god of Kulu and so to his patron the Raja.† Into their big tent comes the gods of the valley, careering through the crowds, lurching about with excitement on the

---

* Local gods are, however, identified with those of the plains.
† Actually a Rai, one below a Raja.

shoulders of their bearers. Flute and drums herald their approach while dancers strung about with marigold chains keep up a slow back-breaking stomp to the accompaniment of euphonium-sized horns.

It was in 1970 that we made that exhausting journey to Kulu. Since then the Kulu Dussehra has encountered crisis after crisis. In 1971 there was serious trouble, said to be politically motivated, over the processional route to the buffalo sacrifice—how often, even a hundred years ago, trouble started over the routing of processions. The police opened fire, panic ensued. The year 1972 saw Dussehra as usual but Ragunathji was not there, nor were many of his fellow gods. And still there were scandals. The trouble is that what was once a local social and religious event has outgrown itself. The stalls of traders outnumber the tents of the gods and they in turn are now dwarfed by the stage and auditorium constructed for the formalised presentation of local dances. It has become a vast commercial and tourism project. The spontaneity and the abandon have gone. The Folk Festival is taking over.

But if the gods stay away the people will surely still come. This is the last chance to stock up on pots and pans, get rid of a spare bullock and have a sore tooth out before the passes are closed again for the winter. The people from the plains, Sikhs and Hindus, Saddhus and tourists, get together with the people of the hills. All night the talk goes on along with the drinking and dancing. The Kului men invest in a new Himachali cap, a low brimless affair faced with a strip of bright velvet, while the women admire one another's homespun blankets. These are worn rather like the Coorgi sari and are made in a variety of shades just like Highland plaids. Amongst them one may spot the little *jozi*, a jewel-spangled cap with a little tail, of a lady from Chamba or perhaps the long flounced dress of a Rampuri visitor.

Adding to the already varied spectacle will be a large crowd of Tibetans, a sample of those who in 1959 accompanied the Dalai Lama in his flight from Lhasa. His Holiness resides in Dharmsala but his flock is scattered throughout the Indian Himalayas and beyond. Passing through Fraserpet in distant Mysore I remember being intensely excited by the number of Mongol-looking people about; it transpired that there was a large Tibetan settlement camp in the area. As common a sight in any big city as the Kashmir Arts Emporium is the Tibetan jersey seller. Particularly in winter when work in the mountains is scarce, Tibetans are plentiful in Delhi's Connaught Circus, waylaying tourists with a disarming smile and the offer of some bulky knitting or a lively little Tibetan terrier. Just round the corner in Janpath they have their own tourist bazaar full of ancient and not so ancient Buddhist prayer wheels and heavy jewellery. Even in the bazaars of Kulu, Simla and Manali the Tibetans have set up shop. But for all this commercial enterprise they are largely a simple, uneducated people earning a miserable wage by working in road building gangs. At the highest altitudes you find a gang of men, women and children chipping away at lumps of granite or clustered round the inevitable kettle of buttered tea. They are always smiling, always busy and as they walk back to their camp of patchwork tents and tattered prayer flags the knitting needles are clicking away in their gnarled hands as automatically as formerly did the prayer wheels.

Tibetans, like the people of Ladakh or, much farther east, of Sikkim and Bhutan are Buddhist. The Buddha was India's greatest religious leader and Buddhism her greatest contribution to history. From sixth-century Bihar—its name derives from *vihara* a Buddhist monastery—and particularly under the patronage of Ashoka, Buddhism spread south through India to Ceylon. Later it swept north through Kashmir and Afghanistan to Tibet, China, Japan and from Ceylon to South-East Asia. In the process the teachings of Siddhartha Gautama, the Buddha, underwent considerable adaptation. Though Buddhism in India repudiated the caste system and appeared for a time as an opponent of the Brahmin-dominated Hinduism of the Vedas it soon came to be accepted as just another path to salvation. Hindu syncretism simply reabsorbed it. Buddhists would join in Hindu worship and Brahmins would be asked to preside over Buddhist marriages and deaths. Traditional Hindu customs seem to have revived long before Buddhism as a body of doctrine waned in popularity. There was apparently no persecution and the Brahmin revival of the sixth–ninth centuries adopted as much Buddhist thought as it eradicated. By the Middle Ages this process was complete. The Buddha was accepted as just another *avatar*\* of Vishnu and Buddhism, along with Jainism, as just another aspect of Hindu tradition.

The brand of Buddhism which installed itself in Tibet and the Himalayas was a later and very different version. It was not until the eleventh century that Vajrayana Buddhism, 'The Vehicle of the Thunderbolt', was established there. Corrupted by the magical and sexual obsessions of Bengali Tantricism and further debased by the earlier demon worship of the Tibetans it had only a tenuous connection with the lofty idealism of the Buddha's teaching. It is thus not possible to trace between the architectural remains of Buddhism in India and the Buddhists of contemporary India—be they Tibetans or ex-Untouchables—the sort of connection which exists between the Jain temples of Abu and the wealthy Jain merchants of Gujerat or indeed between the Moghul palaces and the depressed Muslim minorities of the North. A glance at the famous Buddhist cave paintings at Ajanta,† all delicate feeling and classical purity, followed by a visit to a Buddhist shrine or temple in the Himalayas with its frightening images and garish colours is proof enough. It is true that the Tibetans have done something to revive interest in the great Buddhist shrines of northern India. Ashrams and monasteries at Boddh Gaya, Sarnath and Sanchi are attracting even Westerners; there may yet be a real Buddhist revival in India. But the only place where one is conscious of a living Buddhist ambience is Darjeeling.

Like Simla in the western Himalayas, Darjeeling in the east claims to be the Queen of the Hill Stations. And like Simla the town itself is full of neo-Elizabethan timbered houses, bandstands, parades, clubs, pretentious hotels, all the paraphernalia in fact of an English seaside resort. Instead of the sea lapping round its cliffs

---

\* Incarnation.

† Near Aurangabad in Maharashtra.

and promenades there is an enormous void at the bottom of which some 5,000 feet down are the Ranjit and Teesta rivers. In the early morning as you sally forth for one of the greatest views on earth the valleys are drowned in swirling mist. Across the chasm some forty miles wide there rises from the mist a vision of ice and snow which rears up into the sky and hangs there suspended like the Taj Mahal. This is the massif of Kanchenjunga, third highest mountain in the world. A good place from which to witness this majestic levée is Observatory Hill. There is no observatory but there is, on its peak, a Buddhist shrine. As you stand amidst the fluttering prayer flags trying to assimilate this fantastic apparition, the sound of a temple gong booms through the mist from somewhere down below. The sun climbs rapidly behind the town and the mist rolls back to reveal a clump of *chortens*, Buddhist memorial structures like gigantic chess men, perched on a ledge above the steeply terraced tea plantations. Farther down a pagoda-like monastery appears, all reds and golds against the vivid green of the tea bushes.

Down in the bazaar the people are predominantly Buddhist. At the Lhasa Restaurant the menu is divided into two sections, pork dishes on one side, beef dishes on the other. Most Buddhists are strictly vegetarian but not so Tibetan Buddhists. It is hard to believe that this is Hindu India or that Darjeeling is now part of West Bengal. Settling to a beef chow mein are a family of prosperous Tibetans. The men wear soft, heel-less boots and their hair is in a long pigtail. Anything from an Australian bush hat to a cloth cap may be on their heads but, whatever it is, it is rarely removed. It gives them a distinctly second-hand look; one is reminded of their not-so-distant cousins, the North American Indians. The Tibetan women on the other hand are like Victorian dolls with their big flat faces and long grey dresses. A little square pinafore of striped material is tied at the waist. Nepalis have something similar but the stripes go to the other way. Some Nepalis, notably the tribal people in western Nepal who migrate in search of work to Himachal Pradesh, seemed to wear the pinafores round their bottoms.

Along the Mall from the Lhasa restaurant is the very much

smarter Glenary's restaurant with its pastry shop and delicatessen below. It is not the sort of place in which one expects to see a cross section of the local population; we were there simply for the food. In the middle of a succulent dish of Chicken Mughlai with *pillau* and *paratha*—Punjabi rather than Buddhist or Bengali fare—a hush descended on the dining-room. The swing doors were thrown open and amidst a flurry of waiters and managers there marched in a most impressive group of people. There seemed to be three couples. Dressed in flowing silks and wearing thick make-up the ladies looked rather like geisha girls except that two of them smoked throughout what proved to be a very long meal. Their men were even more impressive. Tall, very broad and identically dressed they were like visitors from another planet compared to the little waiters. Their heads were bare and hair crew cut above craggy features and wide-set eyes. They wore long voluminous coats reaching to their knees with baggy sleeves and turned-back cuffs. The coats were gathered at the waist with a good foot of material hanging over their belts emphasising their bulk. The colour was slate but the cuffs and knee-length socks were white. They looked like bowmen from the Bayeux tapestry or some order of crusader knights. Fascinated we tracked them from the restaurant to a fleet of new jeeps parked outside the planters club. They tore off in the direction of Kalimpong. The jeeps, it seemed, were all registered in Bhutan. If they looked like bowmen it was not surprising. For the Bhutanese archery is a national sport and the bow the Bhutanese army's chief weapon.

Darjeeling was ceded to the British by the king of Sikkim. For the Sikkimese, Bhutanese and some Nepalis it remains the local metropolis. The bazaars are full of sturdy little men with enormous ears, either Lepchas from Sikkim or Gurkhas from Nepal. Mostly they wear a squashed grey pill-box hat with, for the Gurkhas, a small brooch of the crossed *kukris*, Gurkha knives. Sherpas from the higher regions of Nepal are also well represented. Tensing Norgay, the Everest hero, lives here and runs the mountaineering school. The Bhutanese, once identified, are easy to pick out. At first it seems one is meeting the same one over and over again so uniform is their dress. With the exception of the Gurkhas who are Hindus all these people are Buddhist. Ochre-robed monks and the occasional nun impart to the crowds a sense of quiet industry as they click through their beads or wave their prayer wheels, muttering all the while some mesmerising mantra. The Kashmiri curio shops are full of prayer bells and *tunkahs*, Buddhist religious hangings. As you gaze again at Kanchenjunga over a bough of rhododendron bearing a single deep red blossom you realise that such perfection is real only as the subject of a Zen homily or the model for a Japanese scroll painting.

*       *       *

Just as the Moghuls retired to Kashmir and the Viceroys and their A.D.C.s to Simla, so nowadays, during the heat of May and June and during the monsoon, the hippies make for Kathmandu, the Saddhus for Gangotri or Amarnath and the Prime Minister for a bit of walking around Manali or Naini Tal. For everyone the Himalaya is a good place for reflection and meditation. Even the exhausted traveller is tempted to stretch his two weeks in Srinagar to give himself time to assimilate and digest the experience of India. Out of thousands of villages seen from a bus window or towns from hotel foyers one place thus becomes familiar. One village with its shops, temple, school, dispensary and railway station or one town with its crowded bazaars, its cantonment and its rare havens of peace has to do justice for all others. You begin at last to see a cell of Indian society from within. The farmers and peasants round about may be Muslim, Hindu or Buddhist, Kashmiri, Pahari or Bhoti speaking but the town or larger village is sufficiently uniform throughout India to be representative.

All those clapboard constructions along the roadside which with a sense of misgiving you came to know as shops take on an individual identity. There is one which sells everything from shoe laces to battered paperbacks. Above the counter hangs a portrait, with flowing white beard, of Guru Nanak. The proprietor, of course, is a Sikh and though his stock of unlikely goods is limitless so too is his profit margin. Next door is the Punjabi restaurant or hotel. It does not look much like either. There are a few string beds spread about the forecourt and a few rickety benches and tables but there are also bits of lorry and live chickens. The cooking range is a clay platform with holes from which flames and smoke occasionally appear. It all looks most uninviting. But, once tasted, its specialities of *nan*, black *dhal* and mutton *korma* have you craving to stop at every 'Punjabi Dhaba' in northern India and sadly missing them in the South. Equally inevitable is another restaurant which on acquaintance serves only tea. Its speciality will be sweets, not the gaily wrapped little things one sucks, but big chunky balls and cubes of fudge-like consistency in off-white or yellow. The flies, though not usually reliable, are never wrong about Indian sweets. One learns to treat with great caution anything they disdain. For a light but less sticky snack one moves down the street to a *chat* stall. The *chat* seller may not run to even a clapboard shop. With a small spirit stove and a few big brass bowls he operates on the pavement. Sizzling potato cakes, pyramids of *chana*, a bigger type of *dhal*, or stuffed pastries and deep-fried cauliflower sprigs are cunningly displayed at knee level. A leaf or a page from a school exercise book serve as plates; his prices allow of no overheads.

One discovers that no two vegetable shops in a whole bazaar full of vegetable shops are the same. Each has its specialities and each its clientele. For a local family to switch from one aubergine supplier to another is cause for considerable resentment. It has nothing directly to do with the caste system; it is just that a certain rigidity in social behaviour is expected from everyone at every level. The sweet shop will not rush up a plate of eggs however many are hanging unused in a basket above the counter. Egg dishes are part of the Punjabi hotel's repertoire. The owner of the houseboat in Kashmir, which for some years I have patronised, will shake with fury if I so much as greet one of his fellow houseboat wallahs, though he himself may be on the best of terms with them or even related.

The demarcation and proprietariness peculiar to the Indian

customer-tradesman relationship is everywhere. The wretched *dhobi* is liable to baulk at washing clothes for any but his normal clients and may subcontract sheets and pillow cases to a different *dhobi*. The *pan* seller (*pan* is a concoction of betel leaf smeared with and wrapped round a variety of semi-edible materials to which all Indians are addicted) will consider the suggestion that he stock your favourite brand of cigarette with extreme caution. Would it not be better for you to keep walking until you find someone who already stocks Wills Filter?

As you slip gradually into conformity with their complicated pattern of relationships you discover that the tie between you and the *dhobi* or the *chat* seller is not simply one of supply and demand but of patronage in the grand sense. The *dhobi*'s daughter is getting married, will you contribute? Munshi's tonga (horse-drawn cart) driver was not available so he took a taxi, will you pay the difference? Flattering as it is to feel that the whole community depends on you it becomes hard to distinguish whether your obligation is legitimate or not. You are being drawn into the web but whether as part of it or victim of it is never quite clear.

A letter arrives from the postmaster.

Dear . . .,

I am going to give you a trouble. I hope you will not mind it. Although I tried so many times to talk for this with you in the P.O. But due to heavy rush of Public I could not talk to you frequently. That is as you know that I had appeared in the examination of Inspector, Post Office, held at Dharmsala.

As you are going to M. and will stay there with Raja of M. I had come to know that ―― who is a Member of Parliament is a friend of Raja. Please contact him through Raja that he may help me to get through exam.

I hope that you will surely help me at your utmost.

Yours faithfully, Postman ――

What to do? Do you risk upsetting the flow of your mail for ever or do you take what may prove a fatal step into the web of intrigue?

The worry and insecurity of such a situation is common to every Westerner's experience of India. It has coloured every novel about India from E. M. Forster onwards and embittered many who took the solicitude of their servants or suppliers for simple affection. Europeans and Americans whether as visitors, residents or rulers, have tended to care too much about being liked. It is worth reminding oneself that no relationship in India, whether between husband and wife or tradesman and customer, is based on love or affection. Such concepts are too fickle for a rigid society. Mutual respect based on a recognition of the interdependence of both parties and an intimate knowledge of the legitimate claims they have on one another is what counts. The genius of Indians is that of accepting others, not necessarily of liking them. Refugees from Persia, from Tibet and from East Bengal or Pakistan are tolerated; Christians, Muslims and Anglo-Indians are tolerated; Untouchables and beggars are tolerated; equally birds, animals and insects are tolerated. But of sentiment or affection towards any of these outsiders there is little.

If this makes of Indians—and I am thinking of Indians as a generality, not just the peoples of the Himalayas—a seemingly cold and unfeeling people, nothing could of course be further from the truth. For me the most distinctive trait of the Indian people is their kindness. Not a wishy-washy politeness—in most Indian languages there is no equivalent for our incessant 'pleases' and 'thank yous'—but a warm solicitude comprised of gentleness and compassion.

Untouchability and caste or communal discrimination are not especially kind. But these are group attitudes. The hierarchy of subcastes and communities is not rigid. Each is for ever trying to put one over on its neighbour or do down its opposite number. The kindness of Indians lies in the individual not the group. The caste or community may improve its status but the individual is born into one or the other and, to all intents and purposes, can never change it. His position in society is fixed for good and all; as one man to another he can afford to be tolerant, gentle, passive and kind. It must puzzle many visitors how the Bengali peasant or the Punjabi farmer, so seemingly likeable and easy going as individuals, could have been a party to the 1947 massacres in the Punjab or the 1971 atrocities in Bangladesh. As the member of a community an Indian will frequently express prejudices and hostilities which you know that he as an individual would never condone on the level of personal relations. Fascinating as the Brahmin's, the Muslim's or the Jain's peculiarities may be, it is often their typically Indian characteristics which are the most likeable.

Only the Saddhus, the itinerant holy men of India, can claim to be true individuals, beyond the bonds of caste and community. How many *bhikshus, munis,*\* *sannyasis*, etc., there are is anyone's guess, but at big festivals like the Kumbh Mela at Allahabad they gather in their thousands and descend on the Ganges in hordes as at a gathering of the clans. It's all very traditional. For the ancient Greeks as much as for the modern tourist they were one of India's most striking features. No doubt it was as a Saddhu that Cain wandered through Nod doing his penance.

If one thinks of them as a community they defy all the usual rules. Though noticeable amongst the summer migrants to the Himalayas, they have no particular regional affiliations. There are Saddhus all over India. They are not even necessarily Hindu. Sikh Saddhus, Muslim *fakirs*, Jain monks and even the odd Christian itinerant follow much the same sort of life. They may be from any caste, they may be born Saddhus or become Saddhus. Some wear nothing save a coating of ashes, others an incredibly elaborate collection of robes and ornaments. They may be strict vegetarians or live off rotting carrion. They may have hair to their waists or shave off every hair on their bodies. Some are complete rogues, others extremely pious ascetics. In short they are not a community at all; they are purely individualists.

Being a Saddhu means being outside Indian society, beyond community and caste, to an extent that even the foreigner is not. The prospect of such isolation fills most Indians with terror. Privacy and loneliness are anathema in a society based on the joint

---

\* *Bhikshus* and *munis* are normally Hindu, Jain or Buddhist monks.

family household and the caste and locality. The Saddhu is the exception to every rule, the embodiment of a total reaction to all that is typical of Indian society. Yet he is dependent upon it. One thing do all Saddhus have in common; they rely on the generosity of society. In this unique relationship one has a chance to assess Indian behaviour on the purely individual level. It is as if the strength of group loyalties satisfied a man's need for security leaving him free to shower on the Saddhu, the true individual, a patience, generosity and kindness beyond the understanding of any other nation.

# EPILOGUE

Late on a hot sweaty night in May our taxi tore down the deserted road to the airport. As so often before, we were leaving India in full retreat, slinking away under cover of darkness from the oppressive heat, from sickness and from the feeling that another month could confuse every impression I had formed.

With the first step on to the Jumbo I knew we were making a terrible mistake. India is inexhaustible; I realised that, but I had forgotten how the West's apparent sameness makes it so exciting. One look at the plastic colours, the graceless clothes, the poor complexions, and I remembered. The smiles of the cabin staff were as genuine as formica and as cheerful as a shrink-wrapped salad. The plane took off, the lights dimmed for the artificial night and I collapsed. I wanted back. I wanted the simplicity and sincerity of real people. I wanted to touch a worn grinding stone or a smooth wooden railing. I wanted the gentle colours of saffron, ochre and cinnamon or the warm smells of jasmine, sandalwood and turmeric. Above all I wanted the spontaneity and the unpredictability. Even Indian Airlines suddenly seemed infinitely desirable. The prospect of the unexpected, of being thrown back on to one's own resources, of an untamed way of life—all these were vanishing.

I remembered an elderly couple we had met a few days before on a little station in Punjab. The man, a Sikh, was keen to air his English and his knowledge of world affairs but he wasn't such a big shot. They were travelling third and lunch was some *dhal* and *chapattis* cooked by his quiet little wife and packed in a tiffin box. Mercilessly he pried and probed into our circumstances. Like so many he was, I think, puzzled whether to treat us as sahibs or as hippies. It must be difficult for Indians to understand how the long-haired layabouts on the Benares waterfront manage the metamorphosis into the greying and conservative tour members who troop from a luxury hotel to an air-conditioned bus in the Cantonment. At the time I bitterly resented his inquisition; now I suddenly felt very small. His curiosity was so totally genuine. And after all he too was only classifying just as, for months, I had been.

As a Sikh he presumably belonged to no caste. But like the tribal people of Central India or the Christians of Kerala, the wealthy Parsis or the gentle Jains his position in Indian society was as firmly rooted as if he belonged to a caste. Crewcut and chain-smoking he would still be a Sikh just as a Brahmin remains a Brahmin even after eating a steak. His children would marry Sikhs, his friends would be Sikhs and his food would be Sikh food. For the Indian of whatever caste or community there is no question of a metamorphosis. Where the Indian concept of class differs most noticeably from that of the European is in its lack of competition and the snobbery and affectation which result. There are no fences between one man's land and the next and there are no social barriers between men of different caste. Such barriers are artificial, the product of a competitive society. But in India it's different. They are unnecessary for a man is as surely born to his caste as an animal to its species. To most any change is unthinkable. For social competition or affectation there is no place. The Unseeable Nayadi leaves his bowl at the edge of the field and retreats into cover while his wages are put into it. He is as anxious to remain unseen as the higher castes are not to see him. If he ponders on the injustice of things it is not so much in anger as in envy coloured, perhaps, by a certain optimism about his chances in his next reincarnation. The Untouchable who aspires to Sudra status does so not for himself but for his whole caste. Unilaterally no Indian denies his caste or community for therein lies his security.

Ten minutes out of Delhi and already the generalisations were coming fast and furious. The old India hands, back on their P. & O.'s, had the whole country nicely sorted out before they touched Aden. India teaches you to shun the dogmatic but the lesson is soon forgotten.

Waiting to see if the sleeping pills worked I was wrestling with the connection between Hindu and Indian. Did they have more in common than just the derivation? Through the caste system Hinduism becomes more than a religion, really a way of life. If the bonds of community are as strong for non-Hindus as those of caste for the Hindu majority, then Hinduism is not just the Hindu but the Indian way of life. The two are inseparable. Zoroaster and Ambedkar, Mahavira and Nanak, Siva and the Aga Khan, Christ and Krishna—they are all there side by side in the devotional shops, testimony to an extraordinary eclecticism. Far from resenting the intruders India seems to glory in its own diversity. Refugees, Bengali, Tibetan, Khoja and Parsi, are accommodated. Invaders, Huns, Scythians, Afghans and Mongols, are absorbed. Indigenous peoples, Tribals and Dravidians, are assimilated. Even the visitor finds himself drawn deeper and deeper into the heart of the country. Sensing the Indians' ready acceptance he moves from the cities into the countryside, from the hotels to the ashrams and from the first sweeping impressions into the ever-deepening experience of India.

Within each community he discovers cell upon cell of comparable diversity. To the Indian it is not the dogma or history of his religion, language or race that matters but simply its exteriors. One subcaste differs from another purely in the minutiae of dress, food or trade, rarely if ever in beliefs. Political debate rages not around principles and ideologies but personalities, factions and regional groups. The Hindu, or better, the Indian genius is for endless elaboration, complication and contradiction, something of a contrast to the West's passion for simplification and logic.

All of which, while providing inexhaustible scope for argument, tends to invalidate the hard and fast rule. Ask any two Indians a perfectly simple question and invariably you get two irreconcilable answers. That hank of long hair worn by the orthodox Hindu has as many different explanations as it does names. In India one never gets to the bottom of things.

At the same time there is to Hinduism, or the way Indians live, a certain logic which is worth pursuing. After centuries of decrying the Indian attitude to cattle it is now suggested that perhaps all

# Epilogue

those unowned, unwanted and unslaughterable bulls are not such a bad idea. They die, often inconveniently and invariably through starvation, but whilst they live they consume little besides waste and in return produce a valuable fuel on which millions depend for cooking and warmth. *Lungi, dhoti,* pyjamas and *kurta* only have to be worn to be appreciated as the coolest and most comfortable attire imaginable in a climate like India's. The caste system, as has been noted, has a great deal to be said for it. Even arranged marriages in the context of strict caste observance, the joint family household and the Indian attitude to love are not such a bad idea.

It is as well to look twice at all those shrouded corpses lined up along the platforms of Sealdah station. They may not be dying of starvation. The rooftops of the grandest houses are also strewn with snoring bodies. At least for the hotter months of the year most of the population prefers to sleep outside. On Cochin station most of the platform dwellers were pillowed on substantial wooden chests from which toothbrushes, soap and even the odd Gwalior suit was unpacked at sunrise. To those with a low income accommodation may be less important than having the price of a new sari for mother come Divali.

Just as the poverty is rarely as obvious as it seems at first glance so the absurdities of India are rarely as mad as they look.

Hinduism is a most practical religion with not one but at least twenty good explanations for every quirk. A casual dabble in any of the Sanskrit classics reveals a painful obsession with exactitude comparable to the subtleties of that most Indian of sciences, astrology. One never reaches the bottom of things because if one could it would all be suspiciously simple. Indians learn to accept the complications and the contradictions. It's like that concurrence with endless frustrations or the farmer's resigned yet never defeated attitude to the monsoon. The concept of *dharma* rules out any appetite for the class war, the climate discourages any defiance of the elements and yet Indian passivity goes deeper than this. The diversity and complication of life is itself reason for a certain quiet caution as prudent as it is resilient.

# Epilogue

Perhaps fortunately the pill was taking effect. My meditations tailed off into nonsense and in their place came a rapid slideshow of flashing pictures. I saw a troop of schoolgirls in bright blue dresses picking their way through the coco-nut palms which were green and gold in the setting sun. I saw an old man resting on a stack of hay by the railway. I saw a close-up of his eyes, big, bright and gentle, the eyes of a saint wet with tears and smiling with kindness. Then there was a dead flat sea of tea bushes. Waist-deep in the brilliant green waded a gang of pickers; their blouses were scarlet and maroon. Over the lakes of Kashmir I heard again the mewing of the kites. In some village in the North the silence was heightened by the steady thump of a distant pump-well. There were sunsets of frightening splendour seen through the palm groves of Malabar and there were dawns of dew on the tents and mist in the valleys high on the Dhola Dhar. There were temples and palaces, forests and plains, crowds and faces, endless crowds and faces.

More than its diversity, more than its confusions and contradictions, scenes like these stick in the mind. The experience of India is punctuated by moments of such intense and arresting beauty that all else, poverty, heat and sickness, are forgotten. As the experience crystallises, a hard crust of opinion and theory closes over the variety and fascination of India. Only these scenes and images are left. They grow sharper and brighter. Significantly one forgets who or where they are. They are just scenes of India and Indians, a place apart and a people all of whom belong there.

# SELECT BIBLIOGRAPHY

1. *FOR THE TRAVELLER IN INDIA*

BASHAM, A. L. *Wonder that was India*. London 1954.
GEE, E. P. *Wild Life of India*. London 1969.
Murray's *Handbook for Travellers in India and Pakistan, Burma and Ceylon*. London 1968.
Newman's *Bradshaw of Indian Railways and Airlines*.
SALIM ALI. *Handbook of the Birds of India and Pakistan*. Natural History Society 1968–1972.
Plus a selection of novels from below.


2. *FURTHER READING*

BOUGLE, C. *Essays on the Caste System*. Cambridge 1971.
BOUQUET, A. C. *Hinduism*. London 1966.
*Cambridge History of India*.
CARSTAIRS, G. M. *Twice-Born*. London 1968.
GASCOIGNE, A. B. *The Great Moghuls*. London 1971.
GHOSH, J. C. *The Bengali Renaissance*. London 1948.
HOLROYDE, P. *Indian Music*. London 1972.
HUTTON, J. H. *Caste in India*. London 1951.
ISAACS, H. *India's Ex-Untouchables*. Asia Publishing House 1966.
KIPLING, J. L. *Beast and Man in India*. London 1891.
MASON, P. (ed.) *India and Ceylon: Unity and Diversity*. London 1967.
MOORHOUSE, G. *Calcutta*. London 1971.
NAIR, K. *Blossoms in the Dust*. London 1961.
NEHRU, J. *Discovery of India*. Asia Publishing House 1965.
SINGH, KHUSHWANT. *History of the Sikhs*. Princeton University Press 1967.
——*Ranjit Singh, Maharaja of the Punjab 1780–1839*. London 1963.
TODD, Lt.-Col. J. *Annals and Antiquities of Rajasthan*. London 1920.
WOODCOCK, G. *Kerala: Portrait of the Malabar Coast*. London 1967.

# Select Bibliography

## 3. SOME INTERPRETATIONS OF INDIA

CHAUDHURI, N. *Continent of Circe: Essay on the Peoples of India.* London 1965.

KOESTLER, A. *Lotus and the Robot.* London 1966.

MEHTA, V. *Portrait of India.* London 1970.

NAIPAUL, V. S. *Area of Darkness.* London 1964.

SEGAL, R. *Crisis of India.* London 1965.

ZINKIN, T. *India.* London 1963.

BIARDEAU, M. *India.* London 1960.

## 4. SOME NOVELS SET IN INDIA

BANNERJEE, B. *Pather Panchali.* London 1968.

FORSTER, E. M. *A Passage to India.* London 1970.

—— *The Hill of Devi.* London 1953.

GODDEN, RUMER. *Kingfishers Catch Fire.* London 1965.

—— *Two Under the Indian Sun.* London 1966.

JHABVALA, R. P. *The Householder.* London 1960.

—— *A Backward Place.* London 1965.

—— *An Experience of India.* London 1971.

—— *A New Dominion.* London 1973.

KIPLING, R. *Kim.* London 1961.

—— *Plain Tales from the Hills.* London 1964.

NARAYAN, R. K. *The English Teacher.* London 1945.

—— *The Guide.* London 1970.

—— *The Man-Eater of Malgudi.* London 1962.

PREMCHAND. *Godan (or The Gift of a Cow).* London 1968.

RAO, RAJA. *The Serpent and the Rope.* London 1960.

SINGH, KHUSHWANT. *I Shall Not Hear the Nightingale.* London 1961.

# INDEX

197

# Index

Bose, Subhas Chandra, 19, 109, 149–150, 151
Brahma, god, 46
Brahman, the Godhead, 46
Brahmins, 48, 49, 55, 72–73, 78, 100, 121, 169, 174, 180
British,
  treatment of Indian history, 17, 39
  institutions, 35–40
  attitude to princes, 119
  in Kashmir, 170–171, 173–174
Buddha, The, 43, 48, 100, 180, 181
Buddhism, 53
  under Ashoka, 19, 42, 43
  and Jainism, 100
  amongst Untouchables, 129–130
  in the Himalayas, 177, 180–184
Bundelkhand, 136
Bundi, 116
Burhanpur, 30
Burma, 159

Calcutta, 8, 37, 102, 142–152
Calicut, 69
Cambay, 91
Cannanore, 69
Cape Comorin, 69
Cariappa, General, 76
Caste, 47, 48–52, 187, 191–192
  amongst Muslims, 34
  amongst Christians, 71
  in the South, 74–76
  identification, 121–122
  and the tribes, 126
  and the Untouchables, 131
  in Assam, 156
  *See also* Brahmin, Rajput, Vaisya, Sudra, etc.
Cauvery, river, 78
Ceylon, 59, 65
Chaldean Church, 70
Chalukyan empire, 105
*Chamar* caste, 122
Chamba, 179
Chambal valley, 138
Chandigarh, 16, 20
Chandragupta, emperor, 18
Chaudhuri, Nirad, 31, 154
Chauhan Rajputs, 116
Chera kings, 62, 65, 75
Cherrapunji, 160, 161
Chitor, 116

Chola kings, 62, 65
Chota Nagpur, 123, 124, 125
Christians, 68–71, 88, 124, 128
Cinema, Indian, 155–156
Clive, Robert, 19
Cochin, 67–71, 73, 193
Communism, 150–152
Congress Party, 16, 27, 32, 33, 53, 63, 108–112, 119, 130, 151
Conjeeveram (Kanchipuram), 65
Coorg, 76–77
Coromandel coast, 62, 69

D.M.K. party, 63–64
Dalai Lama, 97, 179
Darjeeling, 96, 166, 181–184
Delhi, 7–22, 29, 31, 37, 42, 54, 99, 111, 180
Delhi sultanate, 31, 116
Desai, Morarji, 109
Dharmsala, 179
Dharwar, 75
*Dhobi* caste, 99, 127–128
Digambara sect, 102
Divali, 47, 178
Doab, The, 114
Dravidians, 60–62, 64, 126
Dupleix, 91
Durga, goddess, 47, 54, 126, 143, 178
Durgapur, 51
Durgavati, queen, 125
Dussehra, 178–179

East India Company, The, 39, 92
Elections, 27, 34, 54, 111
Elephanta, 42
Ellora, 42, 100
Ernakulam, 67, 70, 73, 74

Fatepur Sikri, 32, 33, 66
Forward Bloc party, 150
Fraserpet, 180
French ex-colonies, 87

Galbraith, Kenneth, 67
Gama, Vasco da, 68, 70, 91
Gandhi, Firoz, 96
Ghandhi, Indira, 27, 29, 34, 53, 54, 81, 85, 109, 110, 112, 118
Gandhi, M. K. 'Mahatma', 2, 19, 40, 49, 65, 102, 104, 108, 109, 112, 129, 159

# Index

# Index

# Index

# Index